Republic

or

Democracy

Does it Matter

Books by Don Jans

My Grandchildren's America Will it Still be the Land of the Free and the Home of the Brave

Goodbye Constitution, Freedom, America

The Road to Tyranny Individualism to Collectivism

Two Visions of America

Setting Brushfires of Freedom

Republic or Democracy Does it Matter

All Books by Don Jans available:

www.mygrandchildrensamerica.com

www.amazon.com

Republic

or

Democracy

Does it Matter

Don Jans

ISBN   979-8-218-06217-0

COPYWRIGHT PENDING   2022

SMEA PUBLISHING

PREFACE

The United States is in a very precarious position. Every day we lose more and more of our liberties, with many encouraging the government to take them from us. Every day the government exercises another power that was not granted to it in the Constitution. Every day our nation becomes less of a nation with checks and balances and more of a government dominated by our Executive and Judicial branches. Every day our nation becomes less and less of a federalist nation and more and more of a nation with a big domineering centralized government. Every day our nation becomes less and less of a republic and more and more of a democracy.

If you listened to politicians, teachers and professors, journalists, pundits, and individuals from either side of the political spectrum, they would tell you that the United States is a democracy. We constantly hear phrases from both sides of the political spectrum that we must save our democracy, that our democracy is being threatened, that they are the political persuasion that protects democracy, and on and on.

It is rare to hear anybody refer to the United States as a Constitutional Republic, and yet that is exactly how our founders designed us. When we take the time to study history, we learn the discussion of whether we should be a republic or a democracy did take place, specifically during the Constitutional Convention. The founders overwhelmingly endorsed republic and unanimously denounced democracy. They also told us why they made that decision. The very reasons they rejected democracy are raising their ugly head today.

This transformation from republic to democracy is not an overnight sensation. The transformation has been occurring for over a hundred years. It is in the 21st century that the transformation has become indisputable.

If the United States is to remain a free nation, we must remain a republic. I have discussed in this book the differences between a republic, specifically a Constitutional Republic, and a democracy. I have discussed why our founder's endorsed republic and rejected democracy. I have discussed the safeguards the founder's used to keep us a republic. I have discussed the history of the transformation from republic to democracy.

I have also discussed why it is so important that Americans understand the differences between republic and democracy, and why referring to the United States as a democracy is dangerous. Once you understand the differences, it is my hope that you will correct those who incorrectly call the United States a democracy. It is a great way to be about "Setting Brushfires of Freedom."

No book is a work of one person. I have certainly learned this over the years. There are so many people to thank, and I know I will miss a few, so please forgive.

I had no intention of writing another book. I was searching for a purpose. I prayed for several months for God to reveal his purpose, his plan for me. I kept hearing this inner voice say to me whenever I heard somebody say the United States is a democracy, "That is wrong, the United States is a republic, and it was formed as a republic for specific reasons. Americans do not understand this important fact. You should write a book on the topic of republic and democracy." When I finally listened to that inner voice, it all came together.

I called on a special group of people to assist me as I wrote the different chapters. The feedback was critical. The encouragement was critical. Many in this group were the same people who have helped me in the past. Thank you for answering the call once again. Fern Pham, a mother, business lady, and now a registered nurse, willingly and graciously said she would give me feed back again. Wayne Buck, who has also been a key contributor in the past, agreed to read and give feedback again. Cyndi Tingey, another valuable past contributor, willingly agreed to take time to read and give feedback. Mark Roberts was a new contributor and gave great feedback. Thank you Mark, Cyndi, Wayne, and Fern.

The cover turned out to be a family project. Eric, Jenn, Sara, Jadyn, and Jilly all had valuable input. Consequently, there were many revisions, but I am happy with the results. I hope you are as well.

I do hope when you read the book, that you will take the time to do verification and additional research. You will be adventuring into topics that are not taught, not discussed, and in some circles censored. Our founders did their homework. They knew they wanted to form a government that would allow the individual to be free from government restraints as each strived for and achieved their dreams. They wanted to form a government where each individual would never have the liberties endowed on them by the Creator, abridged or infringed by government. They wanted to form a government that would serve the interest of the people and not control the lives, the choices, and the thoughts of the people.

Enjoy the book, learn from the book, and use it as a springboard to understand better what we as a people must do if we are to remain a people free from the constraints and limitations of a large, centralized government.

Table of Contents

Chapter 1. REPUBLIC or DEMOCRACY

Rule by Law or Rule by Majority

Just after the completion and the signing of the United States Constitution on September 17, 1787, in Philadelphia by 39 delegates to what is now known as the Constitutional Convention, as the delegates were leaving the hall, Mrs. Powell asked Benjamin Franklin what type of government the United States had been given. Benjamin Franklin answered, "A Republic, if you can keep it." The United States of American was formed as a Constitutional Republic. No, they did not overlook democracy, they specifically rejected democracy.

Not only was the federal government formed as a Republic, but all the states were guaranteed a Republican form of government as well, so thy would be saved from mob rule that is democracy.

Article IV Section 4 of the United States Constitution:

"The United States shall guarantee to every State in this Union a Republican Form of Government, and shall protect each of them against Invasion; and on Application of the Legislature, or of the Executive (when the Legislature cannot be convened) against domestic Violence."

Even though nearly every politician, teacher, journalist, and citizen call us a democracy and believe that our Founders formed us as a democracy, it is absolutely **NOT** true.

The Founders were learned people. They had studied governments and political philosophers. They knew full well the differences between a Republic and a Democracy, and they repeatedly and emphatically said that they had founded a Republic.

A Republic is a representative government ruled by law. The law is the Supreme Ruler of the land. The law may or may not be written. Our founders determined it is best to write the law, and they did so. We call that document the Constitution of the United States. This makes the United States a Constitutional Republic with our Constitution being the Supreme Ruler of the Land. Our Constitution is our King, our Queen, our Emperor, our Czar.

In a constitutional republic, the elected officials decide on legislation as representatives of the people. In addition to having elected officials, the other primary defining factor of a constitutional republic is a well-defined constitution that limits the power of the government and elected officials and also sets out basic structures, laws, and procedures under which the country is to be governed. The constitution explicitly specifies the rights of the people, and it is to be followed precisely as the people who wrote it intended.

The word democracy is never mentioned in the Declaration of Independence, nor is it ever mentioned in the Constitution of the United States. The founders did tell us why they rejected democracy. They told us it is mob rule, that it is a dictatorship of the majority over the minority, and that it cannot last long. Democracy will be discussed in greater detail in later parts of this book.

Some specific characteristics of a Republic are:

It is ruled by law and not by the whims of a majority.

The law by definition limits the power of the government.

The liberties of the minority cannot be infringed or abridged by the majority. The role of government is to protect the liberties for all.

Rule of Law is upheld, and arbitrary law is rejected.

Each of these characteristics, so fundamental to freedom, will be discussed throughout this book.

John Adams described a constitutional republic as "a government of laws, and not of men". Our Constitutional Republic has separation of powers. This means executive, legislative, and judicial powers are separated into distinct branches of government. There is no single officeholder who has a claim of unlimited power. No single branch of government has a claim of unlimited power. If a single officeholder, or a single branch of government act in such a way as to have a claim or an actual exercise of unlimited power, the Constitutional Republic no longer exists and instead a form of dictatorship would have emerged.

In a constitutional republic, the constitution is the highest power. In all other forms of government, the highest power is held by a group, a branch of government, an individual, someone, or something other than a constitution, with no limitations on their power. These are the differences between democracy, which is a form of dictatorship, and a constitutional republic.

The founding fathers were well read and had studied philosophy as well as government. The Greek philosophers, Aristotle, Socrates, and Plato certainly had an influence on them and the government they created. The founding fathers were also very familiar with the Greek and Roman concepts of government and the influence of Cicero. Early English government and how the

Magna Carta came into play was studied as a symbol of freedom from oppression, The Founding Fathers in 1776 looked to the Magna Carta as a historical precedent for asserting their liberty from the English crown.

Montesquieu's ideas, especially that of balancing power among branches of government, had a prominent influence on the American Constitution. The works and ideas of Thomas Aquinas, Thomas Moore, Thomas Hobbes, Adam Smith, and for sure John Locke had a great influence on the founders thinking and in forming our government including the writing of the Declaration of Independence and the Constitution of the United States. An honest reading of our history and our founding principles and documents can only lead one to conclude that the Bible also influenced every aspect of who and what we are. This part of our history is trying to be rewritten, but the claim that the Bible was not the most important influence in our founding, is without merit.

The founding fathers were well acquainted with republic. They understood unitary republic where there is a single legislative or parliamentary supremacy controlling the government or the nation. England was in the process of adopting a unitary republic with parliamentary supremacy, but adapting it to their limited monarchy. The founders learned that this legislative or parliamentary republic could be as tyrannical as an unlimited monarchy. The founders rejected both, a unitary republic, and a monarchy.

Another form of republic they considered, was a confederated republic known as a confederation of independent states. In this republic, each state retains its independence or sovereignty but joins together with other independent or sovereign states for mutual defense and/or other mutual advantages. This was the form of republic that was adopted by the Continental Congress, when it adopted the Articles of Confederation. The failings of that type of republic were the very reason the founders had gathered in Philadelphia in 1787. Their stated intent for the gathering was to improve on the Articles of Confederation.

Although the stated reason for the meeting in Philadelphia was to improve the Articles of Confederation, some of the delegates, like James Madison and Alexander Hamilton had as their intent to replace the Articles of Confederation. They rejected unitary republic and confederated republic. They were seeking a new type of republic, one that had not yet been invented.

John Adams said, "let us study the law of nature, search into the spirit of the British

Constitution, read the histories of ancient ages, contemplate the great examples of Greece and Rome, set before us the conduct of our own British ancestors, who have defended for us the inherent rights of mankind against foreign and domestic tyrants and usurpers."

There were several factors that led to the Constitutional Convention. The main issue was that the government created by the Articles of Confederation had many weaknesses. It had named the new nation "The United States of America" and it gave congress the authority to make treaties and alliances, maintain armed forces, and coin money. However, the federal government was unable to levy taxes and regulate commerce. This made it very difficult for the federal government to raise money to pay its debts.

By the fall of 1786, the combination of a financial crisis caused by not being able to raise income and thus pay debts, and disorder threatened by dissatisfied farmers in western Massachusetts, led a group of "nationalist" politicians propose that a "general convention" be called for in Philadelphia to address the weaknesses of the Articles. Congress reluctantly agreed to that convention, but limited any actions to the mere "revising" of the existing Articles of Confederation. The fifty-five delegates who met in Philadelphia between May 25 and September 17, 1787, would not only reject the Articles of Confederation altogether, but they would produce the first written constitution for any nation in the history of the world.

Those 55 delegates gathered in the Assembly Room of the Pennsylvania State House during the summer of 1787 faced a formidable task. The thirteen united States were at that moment remarkably disunited. Somehow, in slightly less than four months, these delegates managed to complete an extraordinary accomplishment. The Constitution they drafted has been successful for much of United States history in limiting the power of government on the one hand, and protecting of personal liberty on the other. Among the more than 150 constitutions presently operating in the world today, few have been as successful in creating that delicate balance between governmental power and personal liberty.

This achievement by these delegates was by no means inevitable. Looking back on their work that summer, we can identify a few factors that enabled them to achieve this success. Perhaps the most important factor was the quality of leadership among those most committed to finding a workable solution that had the greatest chance for longevity. The most prominent and most often mentioned would be James Madison from Virginia. Madison possessed a combination of intellect, energy, and political savvy that would lead to abandoning the Articles of Confederation and replacing the Articles with the Constitution of the United States, and at the same time invent this new republic they were seeking.

Madison was joined in this effort by a group of other delegates from Virginia and from Pennsylvania. In a series of meetings before the Convention formally began its business on May 25, this group agreed to a plan not merely to "amend" the Articles of Confederation, but to set the proceedings of the Convention on a far more ambitious course. That Ben Franklin and General George Washington were a part of this group, gave the group both dignity and influence. But it was Madison, James Wilson, and Gouverneur Morris of Pennsylvania who provided the intellectual leadership and who were most committed to creating a national government based on the consent of the people, and not solely the individual states.

On September 12, just five days before the Convention was to adjourn, George Mason proposed that the nearly completed draft of the Constitution be "prefaced with a Bill of Rights." It would, he said, "give great quiet to the people." But the delegates did not embrace Mason's proposal; indeed, when the matter was put to a vote, not a single state delegation supported Mason's proposal. That decision would prove to be one of the most serious mistakes made by the men who drafted the Constitution. When Thomas Jefferson—then serving as ambassador to France—received a copy of the completed Constitution from James Madison, he was unable to contain his unhappiness at the absence of a bill of rights. "The omission of a bill of rights, providing clearly and without the aid of sophisms, for freedom of religion, freedom of the press, protection against standing armies, restriction against monopolies, the eternal and unremitting force of the habeas corpus laws, and trials by jury in all matters," was, Jefferson wrote in dismay to his friend, a grievous error.

When the final draft of the Constitution was submitted to the people of the states for their approval, the absence of a bill of rights quickly emerged as one of the most serious objections to the proposed plan. If many of the supporters of the Constitution subsequently had not promised that they would quickly work to add a bill of rights to the Constitution once the new government commenced operation, it is likely that the document would have failed to gain the approval of the nine states necessary for its ratification. Fortunately, the First Federal Congress of the new government of the United States fulfilled that promise, and in one of its first actions added that bill of rights, making the "more perfect union" devised by the Framers still more perfect. Ironically, the person who took the lead in drafting a bill of rights in the first Congress was James Madison, who had opposed adding a bill of rights not only during the Convention, but also during the debate over ratification in his state of Virginia.

On August 31, the delegates decided (by a vote of eight states to three) that nine states would be appropriate to implement the Constitution among the ratifying states. It was also decided to substitute state conventions instead of state legislatures as the bodies to consider ratification. Delaware and New Jersey ratified the document within a few months after it was sent to them for approval in 1787. Connecticut ratified it early in 1788. New Hampshire became the ninth state to ratify the Constitution in the summer of 1788. On November 21, 1789, North Carolina became the 13th state to ratify the Constitution of the United States.

To answer questions that people might have during the ratification process, James Madison, Alexander Hamilton, and to a lesser extent, John Jay wrote essays that were published. These essays are today called the "Federalist Paper." These essays addressed a variety of issues that were troubling citizens. The "Federalist Papers" appeared to sway many during the ratification process, and they are used as a guide today.

There is no doubt that our nation was intended to be a republic and not a democracy. There is no doubt that our founders intended to limit the power of the government. There is no doubt that our founders intended that the liberties of the people were never to be infringed or abridged, and for sure, not abolished. We know this because they told us in many ways and many forms including writing this in the Constitution itself. As noted before:

Article IV Section 4.

"The United States shall guarantee to every State in this Union a Republican Form of Government, and shall protect each of them against Invasion; and on Application of the Legislature, or of the Executive (when the Legislature cannot be convened) against domestic Violence."

In our Constitutional Republic we have separation of powers. Separation of powers is not a part of a democracy because the majority enacts whatever policy it desires simply by approving it. In a Constitutional Republic it is not so simple. Our Constitutional Republic has separation of powers to ensure discussion takes place to assure that the limitations placed on government are not exceeded and that the liberties of the people are not infringed, abridged, or abolished. Thomas Jefferson reinforced this critical part of republic when in a letter to Judge William Johnson in 1823, he said, "To preserve the republican form and principles of our Constitution and cleave to the salutary distribution of powers which that has established …. Are the two sheet anchors of our Union. If driven from either, we shall be in danger of foundering."

In Federalist 9, Alexander Hamilton discussed the Union as a Safeguard Against Domestic Faction and Insurrection. He praised the constitutional provisions of distribution of powers, checks and balances, and the term of office of judges being during good behavior only. He also commented on elections but noted they were the only democratic activity in the republic.

"The regular distribution of power into distinct departments, the introduction of legislative balances and checks, the institution of the courts composed of judges holding their offices during good behavior; the representation of the people in the legislature by deputies of their own election .... They are means, and powerful means, by which the excellences of republican government may be retained, and its imperfections lessened or avoided." Alexander Hamilton, Federalist No. 9

Some years after the Constitution was ratified, Hamilton wrote an article for a newspaper and noted that the security of the Republic would be as a result of the respect for it. Hamilton believed that this respect would cause the members of the different branches of government to live within its boundaries. "If it be asked, what is the most sacred duty and the greatest source of our security in a Republic? The answer would be an inviolable respect for the Constitution and laws – the first growing out of the last. ...A sacred respect for the constitutional law is the vital principle, the sustaining energy of a free government." Alexander Hamilton, Essay in the American Daily Advertiser, 1794.

In Federalist 1, Hamilton starts the discussion of the Constitution noting how republics, which this government would be, could be overturned, "Of those men who have overturned the liberties of republics, the greatest number have begun their career by paying an obsequious court to the people, commencing demagogues and ending tyrants."

John Adams, in a letter to Mercy Otis Warren noted that republics such as the government that would be formed, needed virtue in the lives of the people, both in their private and public lives, "Public virtue cannot exist in a nation without private, and public virtue is the only foundation of republics. There must be a positive passion for the public good, the public interest, honor, power, and glory, established in the minds of the people, or there can be no republican government, nor any real liberty and this public passion must be superior to all private passions."

John Adams also stated, "They define a republic to be a government of laws, and not of men."

In 1833, Joseph Story, an associate justice of the Supreme Court, stated in his "Commentaries on the Constitution of the

United States," the following, "Republics are created by virtue, public spirit, and intelligence of the citizens. They fall, when the wise are banished from the public councils, because they dare to be honest, and the profligate are rewarded, because they flatter the people in order to betray them."

In Federalist 39 Madison said that the definition of a Republic as the Constitutional Convention held it, "If we resort for a criterion to the different principles on which different forms of government are established, we may define a republic to be, or at least may bestow that name on, a government which derives all its powers directly or indirectly from the great body of the people, and is administered by persons holding their offices during pleasure for a limited period, or during good behavior."

In Federalist 55, Madison makes note to the fact that men are untrustworthy and that a Republican form of government addresses that by creating the controls necessary to hold that depravity in check, "As there is a degree of depravity in mankind which requires a certain degree of circumspection and distrust. So, there are other qualities in human nature, which justify a certain portion of esteem and confidence. Republican government presupposes the existences of these qualities in a higher degree than any other form. Were the pictures which have been drawn by the political jealousy of some among us, faithful likenesses of the human character, the inference would be that there is not sufficient virtue among men for self-government; and that nothing less than the chains of despotism can restrain them from destroying and devouring one another."

In Federalist 14, Madison remarks that the general government of the Republic would actually be limited. It would be limited to those specific items engraved in the Constitution, "In the first place, it is to be remembered, that the general government is not to be charged with the whole power of making and administering laws. Its jurisdiction is limited to certain enumerated objects, which concern all the members of the republic, but which are not to be attained by the separate provisions of any."

A republic limits the power of government. A republic protects the liberties of the people by prohibiting the government from infringing, abridging, or abolishing liberties that the Declaration of Independence understood are endowed to each of us by our Creator. We are a Constitutional Republic. Our founders intentionally, knowingly, formed us to be a Republic. They have stated they did so because as Fisher Ames said, "The known propensity of a democracy is licentiousness which the ambitious call, and ignorant believe to be liberty."

However, today we have people who proclaim to be adherents to limited government and prohibition against infringing or abridging the rights of the people, but still refer to the United States as a democracy, and who voice often that we must save our democracy. These people are doing so because they support all the corruption, depravity, immorality, and eventual tyranny of a democracy, or they do so out of ignorance, that is they do not understand why we were formed to be a republic. These people do not understand the differences between republic and democracy, and they incorrectly equate democracy with limited government, and with individual freedom and liberty.

Chapter 2. **DEMOCRACY**

The origins of the term democracy are often traced back to Ancient Greece. Words ending in 'cracy', democracy is derived from the Greek word kratos, meaning power or rule. Democracy thus means 'rules by the demos' or 'rules by the people.'

Aristotle's definition of democracy was "rule of the many" or majority rule of those who are eligible to vote. All those who are not eligible to vote or are not considered a party of the people, must follow the will of the majority regardless. There are two types of democracies: 1. Direct participatory democracy or direct democracy where all the eligible voters vote for or against the policy in question. 2. Indirect or representative democracy is where the eligible electorate votes for representatives who will then vote on the different policies. Representative government is not unique to democracies. Republics are also a representative government.

Direct democracy would typically exist only in very small population sizes, especially when all the policies or laws are made on this basis. It does exist in some large populations such as California when direct democracy is practiced via propositions, but this is limited in scope as to frequency.

In a democracy, the attitude toward law is that the will of the majority of those eligible to vote and voting shall regulate. There is no regard as to whether this will be determined by deliberation, governed by passion, by prejudice, or by impulse. There is no restraint, and the majority prevails regardless of known or anticipated consequences.

As you will notice, Aristotle mentioned the majority is comprised of those who are eligible to vote. In a democracy, the majority has the power to redefine who is eligible to vote. The majority can redefine the voting group in any way they wish with no restrictions. The numbers eligible to vote typically becomes fewer and fewer as the majority protects its power by eliminating those who they believe do not or will not support their desired policies.

What Plato told us about democracy has been proven.

"When a democracy which is thirsting for freedom has evil cupbearers presiding over the feast, and has drunk too deeply of the strong wine of freedom, then, unless her rulers are very amenable and give a plentiful draught, she calls them to account and punishes them, and says that they are cursed oligarchs[...] In such a state of society the master fears and flatters his scholars, and the scholars despise their masters and tutors; young and old are all alike; and the young man is on a level with the old, and is ready to compete with him in word or deed; and old men condescend to the young and are full of pleasantry and gaiety; they are loath to be thought morose and authoritative, and therefore they adopt the manners of the young."

In Plato's Republic, Book 8 we learn the following:

Plato realized why democracy failed. Democracy inevitably fails because it is predicated not on merit but on popularity. And Plato understood that in a democracy, an ignorant person's opinion has the same weight as that of a learned "master". Plato foresaw that the force of political correctness would have the wise abandoning their wise positions, so they do not suffer from the ridicule, the demonizing, and the intimidation of the less learned or the ignorant.

There is also the threat that if the learned, the wise, are not in the majority position, which they seldom are, the unwise and unprincipled majority can and will eliminate the wise and the learned from those eligible to vote, eliminating any potential influence they might have.

Democracy also fails because it is not politically neutral. You might think that democracy can go either way, left, right, liberal, socialist, or conservative. But democracy is the base of the collectivist ideology. It is the idea that everything should be decided collectively, and that the outcome of that process is binding on every individual, including those who were against it. If the collective dictates that all must conform to the use of certain pronouns, even those who for whatever reason, such as a religious reason would oppose, they would still be compelled to conform.

In a democracy a person is subservient to the wishes or stated needs of the collective, just as with communism and fascism which collectivism is. The individual has only those liberties, such as speech, assembly, and religion, that the collective grants to the individual. The liberties granted do not have to be and seldom are uniform. Liberties are extended based on the group or the individual conforming to the dictates of the collective.

Democracy fails because it is totalitarian and often is despotic. Marx said in the Communist Manifesto that the "Dictatorship of the Proletariat" would have to be despotic to bring about the required changes desired by the collective. With democracy there is no limit on the kinds of questions about which the majority, or the state may decide. Whether it's about working conditions in restaurants, wages, health, education, gender neutral bathrooms, soft drinks in large bottles, smoking in a car, democracies make laws and rules for the situation.

Democracy requires the government to micromanage our lives, to control us, to spy on us, and to steer us, all with the justification that it's in our best interest. Whoever disobeys can expect a fine or imprisonment. No money, property, or individual liberty is safe from the democratic state.

Democracy gains power and retains power because it is a wealth redistribution machine. In a democracy everyone can try to live at other people's expense. People indoctrinated into the collectivist mentality, or those born with a propensity to believe they are owed because they are a victim, vote to put their personal wants, necessities, or dreams, on the collective tab. Power hungry politicians gain power based on the promise of, "Vote for me, and I will take away other people's money and rights in your favor." This redistribution is from the productive and responsible people to the unproductive and irresponsible.

Ancient and modern history shows that democracy leads to moral decline in the society. The redistribution machine, and particularly the welfare state, punishes successful people through higher taxes and gives the money to people who have less. Whatever group you tax, you get less of that group, and whatever group you subsidize you get more of that group. A democracy thus has fewer and fewer producers and more and more takers.

The redistribution machine has proven to promote hedonism, laziness, antisocial behavior, irresponsibility, and discourages virtue. It weakens family ties and the community spirit. It replaces self-reliance with dependency. Dishonest, lazy, or irresponsible individuals are enabled by a welfare state with social workers, subsidies, and benefits. The same rule holds true for parents who raise their children badly, or antisocial individuals who cause trouble. The organizations within the welfare state do not spend their own money but that of others, so they benefit from dependent 'customers'.

People are told that the protection of minorities is a basic principle of democracy. This is incorrect because democracy is about protecting the rights of the majority. The basic principle of democracy is that the majority decides everything. The majority may grant certain liberties to some minorities, but this is subject to fads, not morality. Minority groups that are vocal, intimidating, or aggressive, generally secure more liberties.

At different times in history, we learn that the homosexual community is in favor with the power-based majority, and the Bible believing Christian is detested. The religious liberty of the Christian businessperson will be eliminated as the majority demands the Christian perform duties for the homosexual community despite the teachings of the Bible or face fines and or imprisonment.

Democracy protects the rulers or the government from the people. This would make the rulers or the government the sovereign. In a democracy, it is the majority, or those in power who have total control. They control what will be or will not be investigated, no matter the evidence. In a democracy, it is common for the vote counters to determine the winners of elections. The government determines if election fraud is to be investigated regardless of evidence. The majority or those in power set the agenda and determine what is or is not worthy of investigation.

Democracy, Oligarchy, Autocracy, Tyranny. From better to worst, this is the order in which regimes degrade, as described by Socrates in Plato's Republic. Yet, we are consistently and constantly being told that we must save our democracy. Those that are telling us this, never tell us that Democracy is the forerunner of Oligarchy, Autocracy, and Tyranny. Why did Socrates, arguably the most famous philosopher of all time, think Democracy was so dangerous? Well, Socrates and Plato, in addition to many other prominent political philosophers that followed them, were concerned that democracies are dictatorship of the majority and would lead to a tyranny of the majority, where the majority of citizens oppresses the minority in a democratic state.

The concept of a "superior force of an interested and overbearing majority," as Madison calls it in Federalist Paper #10, has been an inherent flaw of democratic governments long before the founding of the United States. The early democracies of Athens and Rome experienced several moments where a popular tyrant would rise to power appearing to represent the poor "left out" majority, and launch an aggressive campaign in the name of restoring power to the people.

An individual to write about the tyranny of the majority, and to articulate how this concept relates specifically to the United States, is French political philosopher Alexis de Tocqueville, who traveled to the United States in 1831.

He told us, "The American Republic will endure until the day Congress discovers that it can bribe the public with the public's money."

And de Tocqueville said, "Society will develop a new kind of servitude which covers the surface of society with a network of complicated rules, through which the most original minds and the most energetic characters cannot penetrate. It does not tyrannize but it compresses, enervates, extinguishes, and stupefies a people, till each nation is reduced to nothing better than a flock of timid and industrious animals, of which the government is the shepherd."

De Tocqueville added, "It's not an endlessly expanding list of rights — the 'right' to education, the 'right' to health care, the 'right' to food and housing. That's not freedom, that's dependency. Those aren't rights, those are the rations of slavery — hay and a barn for human cattle."

De Tocqueville stresses that democratic societies' dominant feature is the craving for equality, not liberty. Equality is consistent than with democracies and liberty is consistent with freedom.

There are many reasons in a democracy that it goes from a dictatorship by the majority to a dictatorship by fewer and fewer until it is classified as an Oligarchy or becomes a Dictatorship of a single individual. In an early democracy, different political groups with different political goals agree to make compromises that will benefit their group of voters, or constituencies. Eventually these political groups begin disagreeing with each other so much that they no longer believe that compromise with the other group is possible. When the political arena no longer becomes about compromise, it becomes a matter of domination by one group over the other. Because the only limitations or restrictions that are placed on the majority or those in power, are those restrictions and limitations that the majority or those in power place on themselves, that majority or group in power began to limit who can participate. Control and power are held by those chosen by smaller and smaller groups until total power is held by one or a very small group. This is an Oligarchy.

In some cases, democracies fall into dictatorships when "elites" (that is to say, people in powerful positions such as elected political leadership, bureaucrats who hold appointed government leadership positions, or wealthy and powerful business owners and investors) feel that the political system no longer "works" for them; the system is at odds with their interests. As a result, they seek alternatives that will protect their wealth, status, or political influence from being taken away from them.

These "elites" may then take power through a variety of methods. One means is to use democracy against itself. In this situation, a specific party wins an election and then uses its position as the leader of the government to curtail individual liberties and rights, they will often implement arbitrary law and make laws so they can arrest and eliminate political opponents, and they employ the necessary rule of all dictatorships and that is if elections are held, make sure you control the votes by counting the votes. Elections can be controlled through limiting who can be on the ballot, and/or counting the votes the desired way regardless of who was on the ballot.

Democracies will always become ruled by oligarchies or dictators when voters become politically apathetic, thereby withdrawing themselves from participation in the political process. Thomas Jefferson warned us that this would happen even in a republic, when the voters became uninformed, uninterested, and uninvolved.

In classical Athens, commonly referred to as the birthplace of democracy, the political arena, just as in all political arenas, was filled with rhetoric unconstrained by any commitment to facts or truth. The influencers or politicians were focused on controlling the audience's emotions rather than influencing their reason or logical thinking. Power belonged to anyone who could harness the collective will of the voters directly by appealing to their emotions rather than using evidence and facts to change their minds.

Because the only limitations or restrictions that are placed on the majority or those in power are the limitations or restrictions the majority or those in power place upon themselves, those who could most effectively appeal to the emotions of the voters, would secure the power. The less informed, interested, or involved the voters were, the more easily it was to sway them emotionally.

There are also many examples where fear or hate, are used as the tools to appeal to the emotions of the voters. If the voters were convinced they were in danger, and only could avoid the danger if they voted a certain way, they would often cast an uninformed vote. Likewise, if a voter is convinced that other groups of people were a threat to them, the voter would cast an uninformed vote. The aspiring tyrant quickly learned that fear and hate are powerful emotions and throughout history has appealed to these emotions. Democracy is the political system where the gifted orator is most easily able to manipulate their way to power. The gifted orator, through fear and hate, can easily convince the majority that the right to vote must be removed from those groups posing the threat.

Democracies fail perhaps because they are terribly misunderstood. The common understanding is that democracy means freedom. Democracy is dictatorship, it is dictatorship of the majority or those in power, over the minority or those out of power. In a democracy the majority or those in power tell the minority or those out of power how they must live their lives, choices they must make, and how they must think. Democracy requires that all conform to the ideas and demands of the majority or those in power.

With this unrestricted power, the majority or those in power can and do centralize power. They change how laws are made. They negate rule of law and employ arbitrary law, defining the law arbitrarily so they can achieve their desired result, which is generally to punish those who would disagree with them and thus gaining even more power.

Democracy is government with total power and no restrictions, and the people with no liberties or freedoms except those rationed to them by those in power. The ruling majority in a democracy becomes a smaller and smaller number until oligarchy becomes the reality. The number comprising the oligarchy becomes smaller and smaller until autocracy becomes the reality. Tyranny results under both scenarios.

Our Founders rejected democracy because many of them were historians, and they knew that a democracy is a poor model for governance whose goal is liberty.

In a democracy the majority rules. The majority is the law, period.

Thus, the minority will eventually find themselves with absolutely no rights at all. Everything would occur at the whim of the majority, which by now has become those in power.

This is how our founders viewed Democracy.

James Madison, Father of our Constitution, and 4th president did not restrain his feelings about democracy. He said, "Democracy is the most vile form of government. ... democracies have ever been spectacles of turbulence and contention; have ever been found incompatible with personal security or the rights of property: and have in general been as short in their lives as they have been violent in their deaths."

John Adams said, "Remember democracy never lasts long. It soon wastes, exhausts, and murders itself. There never was a democracy yet, that did not commit suicide."

Massachusetts Federalist Fisher Ames said, "A democracy is a volcano, which conceals the fiery materials of its own destruction. These will produce an eruption, and carry desolation in their way."

Benjamin Rush, a Pennsylvania delegate, and a signer of our Declaration of Independence, was short and sweet in his description, "A simple democracy is the devil's own government."

While not a Founder, Noah Webster, who served in the Connecticut Militia and is considered the Father of American Scholarship and Education, put it this way, "In democracy ... there are commonly tumults and disorders ... Therefore, a pure democracy is generally a very bad government. It is often the most tyrannical government on earth."

In Federalist 48 Madison explains that in democracies, emergencies can be used very easily to create tyranny. "In a democracy, where a multitude of people exercise in person the legislative functions, and are continually exposed by their incapacity for regular deliberation and concerted measures, to the ambitious intrigues of their executive magistrates, tyranny may well be apprehended, on some favorable emergency, to start up in the same quarter," Madison wrote.

In Federalist 10 Madison explains other difficulties and dangers of democracy, such as majorities can destroy the rights of the minority, democracies are turbulent and contentious, are violators of property rights and generally end violently. "From this view of the subject it may be concluded that a pure democracy, by which I mean a society consisting of a small number of citizens, who assemble and administer the government in person, can admit of no cure for the mischiefs of faction. A common passion or interest will, in almost every case, be felt by a majority of the whole; a communication and concert result from the form of government itself; and there is nothing to check the inducements to sacrifice the weaker party or an obnoxious individual. Hence it is that such democracies have ever been spectacles of turbulence and contention; have ever been found incompatible with personal security or the rights of property; and have in general been as short in their lives as they have been violent in their deaths."

It can be clearly seen that our Founders did not wish America to be a democracy. They knew the plight of democracy. They knew the weaknesses of the pure democracy, that to which Madison refers in Federalist 10, also extended into representative democracies.

The founders specifically rejected democracy. They gave us their reasons. The founders knew that the majority or those in power had to have limits and restraints. They knew that the rights of the minority had to be protected from the whims of the majority or those in power. The founders understood that democracy is initially dictatorship of a larger majority but that it quickly becomes a dictatorship of the few over the many.

Rule by the majority without limits and absolute protection of liberties for all, is democracy, is dictatorship, is tyranny.

CHAPTER 3. **SUPREME LAW of THE LAND**

"The supreme law of the land" refers to the highest legal power in a nation. Some examples of the highest legal power in a nation would include:

Trajan, who is arguably Rome's greatest emperor and is clearly one of the most significant ancient rulers in history. He expanded Roman rule farther than anyone else in history. Trajan was one of the greatest military rulers, and one of the most philanthropic leaders Rome ever had. Under Trajan Rome prospered. In 117 AD the Senate named him the best ruler.

Alexander III of Macedon, also known as Alexander the Great, is one of the most successful ancient rulers in history. He started one of the largest empires the world had ever seen, and all by the age of thirty.

Charles the Great (Charles I) was the king who laid the foundation for establishing modern countries of France and Germany. He was the King of the Franks, and he is known for uniting the greatest part of Western Europe during his reign in the Middle Ages. He was also King of Italy and the first Holy Roman Emperor.

Napoleon I of France, later known as Emperor Napoleon, was a prominent military and political leader of France and he heavily influenced European politics in the early 19th century.

In addition to the above there are many ruthless Supreme Rulers who expanded the power of their nations and caused the death of many. Never-the-less they were the Supreme Ruler and people quickly learned to not question their authority. This would include the likes of Attila the Hun, Genghis Kahn, Timur, Queen Mary I (Bloody Mary),

Vladimir Lenin, Joseph Stalin, Adolph Hitler, Mao Zedong, Idi Amin, and Augusto Pinochet. I am sure that you have others that you would and could add to these lists, but the point is, these people were the Supreme Ruler of their Kingdoms. Some Supreme Rulers were more benevolent, and others were more despotic. They made rules and laws as they needed them to accomplish their whim at any time. They were individuals, some had committees ruling with them, some had written constitutions, but they all responded as does any dictator, which includes the dictatorship of the majority, and ruled without limitations or restrictions. They also believed that liberties of the people should be rationed based on allegiance and obedience to them.

This is in contrast to the United States, a truly unique nation founded on the principle that In the United States, the supreme law of the land is the Constitution and any Constitutional Amendments. This has been referred to as rule by law and not by man. It is the Constitution, that determines that we are a Constitutional Republic because the supreme law is in writing.

We have learned throughout history that Supreme Rulers have been challenged, some disposed by force, and some eliminated through assassination. When that happened, a new Supreme Ruler was put into place as the supreme law of the land. In the United States today, our Supreme Ruler, the Constitution, is under attack. The enemy of our Constitutional Republic would be those who believe the Constitution should not be the supreme law of the land, but that we should dispose of the Constitution and replace it with rule by the majority or democracy. The majority would become the Supreme Ruler and what the majority would rule would become the law of the land, the same as in any dictatorship.

This transformation is being openly waged. Whoever wins, that is our republic with the Constitution as the Supreme Ruler, or democracy with the majority as the Supreme Ruler will determine whether the United States remains a free nation or becomes a nation where the people are slaves to the demands of a dictator like we saw under the rulers mentioned earlier. How the people are treated will depend upon whether the new Supreme Ruler, the majority, is benevolent or despotic.

It was the intent of our founders that we be a republic. They wrote the Constitution, and we became a Constitutional Republic. There was much debate that took place in Philadelphia that summer of 1787. The need for power to be separated and how best to accomplish this goal was discussed. James

Madison expressed that separation of powers is needed because men are not angels.

The founders were attempting to solve two of the most significant problems in political theory; how to guard against the very people who were created to guard us, or government; and the problem of keeping a government with limited powers, limited to those powers over time. The solution the Founding Fathers came up with was one taken from the thoughts of Montesquieu, namely, "separating the powers" of the state into different "branches" with the intention that each different branch, jealous of its own powers, would keep the other branches limited in their powers.

Montesquieu in his book, "The Spirit of the Laws (1748)" stated that in order to avoid dictatorship and abuse of government power, it is important to divide the functions and responsibilities of the government and give those responsibilities to different people so that one man will not have total control over a state."

In The Federalist No. 47, James Madison wrote that "the preservation of liberty requires that the three great departments of power should be separate and distinct." Why? Because the "accumulation of all powers, legislative, executive, and judiciary, in the same hands, whether of one, a few, or many, and whether hereditary, self-appointed, or elective, may justly be pronounced the very definition of tyranny."

Dividing powers among different branches of government, he argued in The Federalist No. 51, gives "those who administer each department the necessary constitutional means and personal motives to resist encroachments of the others."

Critical to the separation of powers doctrine is federalism. Federalism is the other safety precaution built into the Constitution by the Founders. The Constitution gives limited powers to the national government, and reserves the remaining power of government to the independent, sovereign states of the Union. This arrangement avoids having a centralized, all-powerful national government, and it's just as essential to the preservation of liberty and freedom as is the separation of powers within the national government.

The Constitution addresses the Legislative Branch of government in Article I, the Executive Branch of government in Article II, and the Judicial Branch of government in Article III. It is in the 10th Amendment that federalism is directly addressed, "The powers not delegated to the United States by the Constitution, nor prohibited by it to the States, are reserved to the States respectively, or to the people." The powers delegated to the United States by the Constitution are found in Article I and Section 8.

In Article 1, Section 8 of the United States Constitution, 17 Congressional powers are listed. Specifically, Congress has to power to:

"Lay and collect Taxes, Duties, Imposts and Excises, to pay the Debts and provide "for the common Defense and general Welfare of the United States; but all Duties, Imposts and Excises shall be uniform throughout the United States.

Borrow Money on the credit of the United States.

Regulate Commerce with foreign Nations, and among the several States, and with the Indian Tribes.

Establish a uniform Rule of Naturalization, and uniform Laws on the subject of Bankruptcies throughout the United States.

Coin Money, regulate the Value thereof, and of foreign Coin, and fix the Standard of Weights and Measures.

Provide for the Punishment of counterfeiting the Securities and current Coin of the United States.

Establish Post Offices and post Roads.

Promote the Progress of Science and useful Arts, by securing for limited Times to Authors and Inventors the exclusive Right to their respective Writings and Discoveries.

Constitute Tribunals inferior to the supreme Court.

Define and punish Piracies and Felonies committed on the high Seas, and Offences against the Law of Nations.

Declare War, grant Letters of Marque and Reprisal, and make Rules concerning Captures on Land and Water.

Raise and support Armies, but no Appropriation of Money to that Use shall be for a longer Term than two Years.

Provide and maintain a Navy; to Make Rules for the Government and Regulation of the land and naval Forces.

Provide for calling forth the Militia to execute the Laws of the Union, suppress Insurrections and repel Invasions.

Provide for organizing, arming, and disciplining, the Militia, and for governing such Part of them as may be employed in the Service of the United States, reserving to the States respectively, the Appointment of the Officers, and the Authority of training the Militia according to the discipline prescribed by Congress.

Exercise exclusive Legislation in all Cases whatsoever, over such District (not exceeding ten Miles square) as may, by Cession of particular States, and the Acceptance of Congress, become the Seat of the Government of the United States, and to exercise like Authority over all Places purchased by the Consent of the Legislature of the State in which the Same shall be, for the Erection of Forts, Magazines, Arsenals, dockyards, and other needful Buildings; And

Make all Laws which shall be necessary and proper for carrying into Execution the foregoing Powers, and all other Powers vested by this Constitution in the Government of the United States, or in any Department or Officer thereof."

Those who believe in unlimited government, those who believe in democracy, have justified the federal government exceeding the specific powers granted to them in the

Constitution by using the "general welfare" phrase as a catch all. To justify their unconstitutional actions, they have greatly enhanced the clauses "to promote the general welfare" and "to make all laws which shall be necessary and proper."

James Madison disagrees with those who claim the general welfare comment gives virtually unlimited power. He clarified this when he wrote, "With respect to the words "General welfare" I have always regarded them as qualified by the detail of powers connected with them. To take them in a literal and unlimited sense, would be a metamorphosis of the Constitution into a character, which there is a host of proofs was not contemplated by its Creators."

Madsion further explained how a misinterpretation of general welfare would further erode the intent of limiting government when he said, "...for if the clause in question really authorizes Congress to do whatever they think fit, provided it be for the general welfare, of which they are to judge, and money can be applied to it, Congress must have power to create and support a judiciary establishment, with a jurisdiction extending to all cases favorable, in their opinion, to the general welfare, in the same manner as they have power to pass laws, and apply money providing in any other way for the general welfare....

If Congress can employ money indefinitely to the general welfare, and are the sole and supreme judges of the general welfare, they may take the care of religion into their Own hands; they may appoint teachers in every state, county, and parish, and pay them out of their public treasury; they may take into their own hands the education of children, establishing in like manner schools throughout the Union; they may assume the provision for the poor; they may undertake the regulation of all roads other than post-roads; in short, everything, from the highest object of state legislation down to the most minute object of police, would be thrown under the power of Congress; for every object I have mentioned would admit of the application of money, and might be called, if Congress pleased, provisions for the general welfare."

And yes, congress is attempting to take the care of religion into their own hands. Yes, Congress has taken control of the education of the children. It would be correct to say that according to James Madison, the Father of the Constitution, the Department of Education, and all affiliated actions would be exceeding the powers of the federal government as intended in Article 1, Section 8 of the Constitution. This would also apply to the welfare system and to the regulation by the Department of Justice of local police forces.

According to the Father of the Constitution, the General Welfare clause does not give power or permission for federal involvement in the internal affairs of the States. There is no provision in the Constitution for federal power over parks, schools, preserves, police, hospitals, healthcare, or the myriad of other "programs" funding which use the "general welfare clause" as a justification for the increase of their power. And to the contrary, once we see the adoption of an erroneously expansive interpretation of the General Welfare clause, and see federal involvement in our schools, local governments, parks, preserves, police, roads, and every minute affair of our lives, we will know we have an absurdly out of control federal government, a federal government that has greatly exceeded its Constitutionally limited powers.

As Madison himself said, "I venture to declare it as my opinion, that, were the power of Congress to be established in the latitude contended for, it would subvert the very foundations, and transmute the very nature of the limited government established by the people of America; and what inferences might be drawn, or what consequences ensue, from such a step, it is incumbent on us all to consider."

Our congress has explicitly stated over the years that it disregards our formation as a republic with the Constitution as the Supreme Ruler of the land and it has placed itself as Supreme Ruler. Our congress has explicitly stated that it dishonors our republic and will be complicit in the stated effort to transform our republic into a democracy. Departments such as the

Department of Education, Department of Health and Human Services, The National Park Service, welfare services of any kind, and many others violate the Constitution of the United States. If Congress believes these are services that the government must provide, they should amend the Constitution per Article V of the Constitution.

Article I, Section 1 of the Constitution of the United States:

"All legislative Powers herein granted shall be vested in a Congress of the United States, which shall consist of a Senate and House of Representatives."

Article !!, Section 1 of the Constitution of the United States:

"The executive power shall be vested in a President of the United States of America."

Article III, Section 1 of the Constitution of the United States:

"The judicial power of the United States shall be vested in one Supreme Court, and in such inferior courts as the Congress may from time to time ordain and establish."

Each branch of government was assigned specific powers. This is critical to a limited government where the branches of government are independent from one another. The branches of government are not necessarily equal, and the founders did not intend for our branches of government to be equal, but they did specifically institute checks and balances on each of the branches by the other independent branches.

In Federalist 78 Hamilton acknowledges that the Judicial Branch would be the weakest branch when he wrote, "It proves incontestably, that the judiciary is beyond comparison the weakest of the three departments of power; that it can never attack with success either of the other two;

and that all possible care is requisite to enable it to defend itself against their attacks." However, we could successfully argue that the Supreme Court has become the strongest branch as it has given itself powers beyond the intent of the founders.

For instance, the concept of judicial review (judicial veto) is nowhere mentioned in the Constitution of the United States. It was imposed upon the Constitution by John Marshall, in the famous case Marbury v. Madison in 1803.

Thomas Jefferson's view was that if the Founding Fathers had wanted to give the Supreme Court the power of judicial review, they would have written that power into the Constitution. He regarded Marshall's decision in Marbury v. Madison as a kind of silent junta that overthrew the clear intentions of the Constitution. Some would contend that the consequence of this decision is that the Supreme Court made itself the most powerful branch of government.

The legislative branch, which was intended to be the most powerful branch of government, because it was the closest to the people, was the sole branch specifically given the duty to legislate. To legislate means to make laws, and in our republic to make laws within the specific limited powers granted by the people to the government as stated in Article I Section 8. The language of the text in Article I Section 1 grants all of the legislative authority of the Federal Government to the United States Congress. the legislative powers given to Congress cannot, or should we say constitutionally cannot be exercised or employed by the President because he is the executive branch, or to the courts because they are the judicial branch.

Any legislation, or making of laws by the executive branch, be it in the form of regulations or executive orders, would be prohibited by the Constitution of the United States. The main difference between a law and a regulation is that the law is supreme whereas the regulations are subordinate and supplemental in nature. If and when the regulation expands or contracts the law, the regulation then takes on the nature of being a law itself.

The Environmental Protection Agency is a part of the Executive Branch that has been accused of exceeding its regulatory authority and has taken upon itself to make law. The EPA's Clean Water Act is one example, whereby the federal government via the EPA has staked its claim to hundreds of waterways around the country in the name of "clean water," from public lakes to ponds on private property. By expanding the definition of "waters of the United States" (WOTUS), the EPA has seized the power to slam private landowners with more permits and higher compliance costs, including major fines.

One family in Wyoming was hit with a $75,000-per-day fine for building a pond on their own property.

As if that wasn't enough, the EPA is now going after farmers for tending their land, not public property, but their own farmland. The federal agency sent a vine and wheat grower in California a cease-and-desist letter ordering suspension of farming operations on a small parcel of land in rural Tehama County. The EPA claimed that the framer had broken the law under the new WOTUS rule, putting "clean water" in jeopardy.

The offense, plowing his own land. And he wasn't even given the chance to contest the EPA's allegations. The Farmer had to go through a lengthy legal battle to reclaim the right to work his land in peace.

In another example, a group of states, energy companies, and business interests stated a key climate change rule exceeded the authority given to the EPA by Congress. At issue was EPA's regulation that set limits on the amount of carbon dioxide that could be released from newly built coal, and natural gas-fired power plants, based on the amount of electricity they produce.

The group contended, "In adopting the rule, EPA far exceeded the authority provided by Congress under section 111(b) of the Clean Air Act to set emission standards for new fossil-fuel-fired steam generating units." That the EPA was legislating and not regulating was charged. This charge has been leveled against the EPA often as well as against other agencies.

There is no explicit definition in the U.S. Constitution of executive orders, proclamations, and presidential memoranda. Thus, there is no provision authorizing their issuance. The president does not have any power or authority to create law. Executive orders and memoranda must conform to law. It cannot be stated enough, the president does not have any power or authority to create law.

A president's executive order for mandatory vaccinations, or testing mandate for large businesses, was struck down by the U.S. Supreme Court, saying it would represent a "significant encroachment into the lives and health of a vast number of employees."

The justices said, "Although Congress has given OSHA the power to regulate occupational dangers, it has not given that agency the power to regulate public health more broadly. Requiring the vaccinations of

84 million Americans, simply because they work for employers with more than 100 employees, certainly falls in the latter category."

The U.S. Supreme Court again made it clear that presidential executive orders are not laws and cannot be enforced as such. The same reasoning would prevail in all categories including immigration, border protection, fossil fuel exploration and extraction, the nation's economy, and family life.

Only congress has the constitutional right to make law. Congress abdicates its constitutional duty when it passes a law in concept, such as the Affordable Care Act, and then directs the agencies to write regulations that in fact define the law. Congress has no authority to pass its power to legislate to either the executive branch or the judiciary branch.

The United States Constitution, the Supreme Law of the Land states who has control over elections. Article I Section 4 states, "The Times, Places and Manner of holding Elections for Senators and Representatives, shall be prescribed in each State by the Legislature thereof; but the Congress may at any time by Law make or alter such Regulations, except as to the Places of choosing Senators."

Authority over elections cannot come under the rule of federal courts, state courts, state officials, county officials, or anybody but the state legislators with the exception being the Congress of the United States. Any alteration to this clause, even in the case of a real or perceived national emergency such as a pandemic, would render the election to be unconstitutional and thus it would be null and void. This would be true with or without widespread voter fraud that may result because of the unconstitutional changes to the rules and laws as stated in Article 1 Section 4 of the United States Constitution.

Article VI Section 2 or the United States Constitution states, "This Constitution, and the Laws of the United States which shall be made in Pursuance thereof; and all Treaties made, or which shall be made, under the Authority of the United States, shall be the supreme Law of the Land; and the Judges in every State shall be bound thereby, any Thing in the Constitution or Laws of any State to the Contrary notwithstanding."

Executive orders, regulations of agencies, or court opinions are not included in the definition of supreme Law of the Land. This is despite people referring to them as such. No branch of government, not even we the people, has greater authority than does the United States Constitution. We are a republic and not a democracy.

A law passed by congress with a majority or even a super majority, an executive order, a regulation, a court opinion, a declaration by an oligarchy, or even a majority vote by the people does not make an unconstitutional act legal. Congress, the executive branch, the judicial branch, and the people still have to operate within constitutional boundaries that were established by our founding fathers, via our founding document, The Constitution of the United Staes. Yes, we were formed as a Constitutional Republic where the Constitution of the United States is the Supreme Law of the Land.

CHAPTER 4. **UNLIMITED POWERS**

The purpose of the Constitution of the United States was to limit the power of the government and to protect the liberties of the people.

"The two enemies of the people are criminals and government, so let us tie the second down with the chains of the Constitution so the second will not become the legalized version of the first." Thomas Jefferson

James Madison writes in Federalist 51 that "Men are not angels; their passions and self-interest often get the better of their reason and sense of justice, so we need government in order to protect our rights against those who would take them away". "But for the same reason," Madison writes, "government must be limited because people in government have passions and interests too."

When the phrase "limited government" is used, it refers to any central government in which that government's powers over the people are limited by a written or otherwise agreed to constitution or overriding rule of law. In the United States we have a Constitution. This would be in contrast to having no constitution or overriding rule of law and the government, the majority, or those in power had no restraints or limitations on their authority. They would have no defined powers such as we find in Article I Section 8 of the Constitution. The government, the majority, or those in power would have absolute power. The government, the majority, or those in power would have dictatorial powers, and nobody would have the right to object.

Totalitarianism would be a form of government that has no limitations on its power. The ruling entity recognizes no limitations whatsoever on its power, including of its citizens' lives or rights. Any objection to or criticism of the ruling entity, or protest against its policies are crimes and punishable in any way determined by the ruling entity, including death. The protection of due process does not exist.

Democracy is a form of government that allows the people to choose leadership within the rules established by the majority. The generally stated goal is to govern through fair representation and prevent abuses of power. To accomplish this stated goal there would need to be discourse, debate, and compromise to satisfy the broadest possible number of public interests. Democracies generally begin and most often continue to claim they advocate for fair and free elections, civic participation, human rights protections, and law and order. Fair and free elections, civic participation, human rights protections, and law and order become what the majority or those in power define them to be.

Majority rule is consistent within a democracy, but the question that must be asked is, the majority of what body. For example, in Athens in the middle of the 4th century, there were about 100,000 citizens (Athenian citizenship was limited to men and women whose parents had also been Athenian citizens), about 10,000 "resident foreigners," and 150,000 slaves. Out of all those people, only male citizens who were older than 18 were a part of the demos, meaning only about 40,000 people could participate in the democratic process. In a population of 260,000, 20,001 supposedly determined the laws of the city.

In the Athens Democracy, the Assembly was the governing body. They would hold meetings about 40 times a year and any of the 40,000 men who were eligible to vote could attend. Only about 5,000 men attended each session of the Assembly; the rest were serving in the army or navy or working to support their families. That means that 2,501 dictated the laws of Athens which had a population of 260,000. Oligarchy is government by a few. You decide if that would be rule by oligarchy.

Just as in Athens, there are voting requirements in all democracies. South African citizens, over 18 years of age, who have registered as a voter and hold a national identity book for the purpose of proof of identity can vote. People who have not bothered to register, or who cannot prove their identity may not vote.

Australian citizens 18 years and over are not only eligible to vote, but legally required to do so. British subjects who were on the electoral roll before January 26, 1984, are also allowed to vote. A prisoner serving a sentence of five years or more, or a person with a standing conviction of treason, may not vote.

In Canada, to register and vote in a federal election, you must be a Canadian citizen aged 18 or older on election day and provide acceptable proof of identity and address.

The voting requirements in Germany after World War I, allowed women to vote for the first time and lowered the voting age from 25 to 20 and citizenship was required. In the 1936 elections, the citizenship requirement remained but Jews and other ethnic minorities were excluded because their citizenship had been removed.

The phrase that the majority rules in a democracy, is meaningless. The critical question to ask is the majority of what body, or who is eligible to vote. In a democracy, where there are no limits on the power of the majority, that defined majority can, and often does, redefine the eligible voting body.

Over the last one hundred years, representative democracy has become the most common type of government across the world. More than half of the countries on Earth claim to be democracies. This claim would mean that the general population has the right to vote and participate in politics by electing political representatives to act on their behalf.

However, despite representative democracy's popularity around the globe, it is important to remember that democracies can easily fail without proper upkeep. Our founders rejected democracy because they told us that democracy is just another form of dictatorship. Again, they were correct as we have seen many countries such as Venezuela, Nicaragua, Egypt, and many others become full-fledged dictatorships.

So how exactly does a democracy become a dictatorship? There are many ways, but there are three general ways. One is where the competing political sides no longer want to cooperate with one another, allowing violent or extremist groups to take over politics instead. It also occurs when a country's elites feel that democracy no longer "works" for them. When these elites feel that losing an election may mean forfeiting their power and influence over the country, they may seek to take over the country by force, turning it into a dictatorship. Or, democracies can fall the other or more subtle way, when elites first grab on to power via democratic means, before they strip away the liberties and rights of the people. Democracies also fall into dictatorships when voters become politically apathetic, thereby withdrawing themselves from participation in the political process, or as Jefferson said, "people become uninterested, uninformed, and uninvolved."

Here is a sample list of dictatorships that did arise from a democracy: Poland: 1926-1989, Germany: 1933-1945, Austria: 1933-1945, France: 1940-1945, Spain: 1939-1976, Brazil: 1964-1985, Chile: 1973-1990, Nicaragua: 1979-1990, 2006-Present, Venezuela: 2002-Present.

In the United States today there are more than 400 federal agencies that issue thousands of regulations controlling every aspect of our lives, from our air and water to our farms and factories. The executive branch now chooses which laws to enforce and issues its own laws through executive orders and administrative rules. And the federal courts now routinely decide matters of public policy historically and constitutionally reserved to the states, including life, marriage, and morality. When we review Article I Section 8 of the Constitution, there is not a power given to the federal government to decide those matters.

Woodrow Wilson receives much of the credit for advancing the progressive administrative state, what has now become known as the "deep state", or that part of government that does not have to be nor are they responsive to the public. Wilson had an infatuation for the British constitutional system, in which the role of government is not laid out in a single written document but instead comes from an ever-evolving set of laws and judicial precedents that are contingent on historical progress. As a college senior, Wilson wrote an article entitled, "Cabinet Government in the United States," proposing that the American separation-of-powers system be replaced by a parliamentary model.

When Wilson entered politics, in his campaign for governor of New Jersey, he raised concern, I guess not enough, by pledging to become an "unconstitutional governor," by which he meant that he had no intention of keeping to the role outlined for the chief executive under the separation of powers. For Wilson, the separation of powers was the source of much of what was wrong with American government.

Based on Wilson's disdain for the separation of powers, his disdain for the Constitution of the United States, and his objection to the Founders' understanding of limited government and unlimited liberty, Wilson put forth a series of institutional proposals designed in one way or another to overcome what he considered to be obstacles to his ideas of unlimited government and limited liberties. Wilson believed the president must not be confined to the constitutionally defined powers and duties of the executive as stated in Article II of the Constitution, because it is too limiting.

Under the Wilson Administration more progressive policies increasing government influence over the lives of Americans were instituted. Government also massively expanded in its size, scope, and power. In 1913 federal spending per person was $27.55, in 1916 federal spending per person was $83.60, and by 1919 it had risen 16-fold, to $1,329.77.

Wilson's progressive era, saw federal power advanced in unprecedented ways. The railroads were nationalized, waterborne shipping was regulated, and the United States Food Administration, was created in 1917, controlling all aspects of the food industry, from agriculture to distribution to sales. Similar regulation was applied to fuels, and eventually to the whole economy. When the federal income tax was introduced in 1913, the highest tax bracket was 7 percent for all income above $20,000. By 1918 the highest rate rose to 77 percent beginning at $4,000.

Wilson said that a new understanding of government was necessary. This new understanding required an evolutionary understanding of the Constitution, an understanding in which government is determined by looking not to the Constitution as written, but instead to the new demands placed upon government by current circumstances.

In his New Freedom campaign for President in 1912, for instance, Wilson urged that the rigid, mechanical, "Newtonian" constitutionalism of the old liberalism be replaced by a "Darwinian" perspective, adjusting the Constitution as an organic entity to fit the ever-changing environment.

Wilson also blamed separation-of-powers theory for what he believed to be the inflexibility of national government and its inability to handle the tasks required of it in the modern age.

Wilson said, "The trouble with the theory is that government is not a machine, but a living thing. It falls, not under the theory of the universe, but under the theory of organic life. It is accountable to Darwin, not to Newton. It is modified by its environment, necessitated by its tasks, shaped to its functions by the sheer pressure of life. No living thing can have its organs offset against each other, as checks, and live."

Wilson saw the separation of powers as a hindrance because efficiency was to be valued over anything else. The growth of the administrative state, or rule by bureaucracy and not by elected officials, and treating the presidency as a prime minister, caused a dramatic rise in the size and power of government. It also brought about a deterioration of the separation of powers.

In Wilson's first year in office, he signed The Federal Reserve Act of 1913 which established the Federal Reserve System as the central bank of the United States. The U.S. Constitution does not mention a central bank, nor does it grant the government the power to create one. Thus, government does not have any authority to create a federal reserve bank because it is not one of the Enumerated Powers of Congress. A constitutional amendment would be required.

Wilson insisted on the passage of The Sedition Act of 1918, which passed as an amendment to the already instituted Espionage Act of 1917, which increased government surveillance of citizens and put a cap on speech that was deemed to profane government, even though it was a clear violation of the First Amendment. Agencies such as the War Industries Board, which greatly enhanced the federal government's ability to regulate industry were established. Created by executive orders rather than congressionally approved legislation and law, the WIB lacked the political and legal power to fully centralize industrial mobilization.

Woodrow Wilson desired to transform the United States from a republic to a democracy. He despised our Constitution, the rule of law, the separation of powers, limited government, and unlimited liberties. It was under Wison that democracy took a giant step forward and with a move to democracy, the peoples liberties were now challenged. A serious deterioration of individual liberty was under way.

Dictatorship, known as democracy, became more and more accepted.

Many Americans have forgotten the enormous damage to the United States Constitution and our Republic the progressive years of Woodrow Wilson caused.

Although Wilson certainly instituted the administrative state and the imperial presidency, Franklin Roosevelt took it to heights Wilson probably never imagined.

When Franklin Roosevelt ran for president in 1932, he did so on a Democratic Party platform that many "Freedom Loving Americans" would gladly support. The platform said that the federal government was far too big, taxed and spent far too much, and intruded in the affairs of the states to too great an extent. It said government spending had to be cut, taxes reduced, and the federal budget balanced. It called for free trade and a solid gold-backed currency.

But as soon as Roosevelt was inaugurated in March 1933, he instituted a series of programs and policies that turned all those promises upside down. Yes, he lied. In FDR's first four year in office, taxes were increased from a top tax rate of 63% to 79%, government spending reached heights never seen before in U.S. history going from $4.2M in 1932 to $9.2M in 1936, and the federal budget bled red with deficits as it increased from just over 20% of GDP in 1932 to over 40% of GDP by 1936. The bureaucracy ballooned; public-works projects increasingly dotted the land; and the heavy hand of government was all over industry and agriculture. The United States was taken off the gold standard, with the American people compelled to turn in their gold to the government for paper money under the threat of confiscation and imprisonment.

In June 1933 Congress passed the National Industrial Recovery Act (NIRA), after which FDR created the National Recovery Administration (NRA). Modeled on Mussolini's fascist economic system, it forced virtually all-American industry, manufacturing, and retail business into cartels possessing the power to set prices and wages, and to dictate the levels of production. Within a few months, over 200 separate pricing and production codes were imposed on American business. The symbol of the NRA was a Blue Eagle that had lightning bolts in one claw and an industrial gear in the other. Every business in the country was asked to have a Blue Eagle sign in its window that declared, "We Do Our Part," meaning it followed the pricing and production codes. Citizen committees were formed to spy on local merchants and report if they dared to sell at lower prices.

Propaganda rallies in support of the NRA were held across the country. During halftime at football games, cheerleaders would form the shape of the Blue Eagle. Government-sponsored parades featured Hollywood stars supporting the NRA. At one of these parades the famous singer Al Jolson was filmed being asked what he thought of the NRA; he replied, "NRA? NRA? Why it's better than my wedding night!" Film shorts produced by Hollywood in support of the NRA were shown in theaters around the country; in one of them child star Shirley Temple danced and sang the praises of big-government regulation of the American economy.

The NRA codes were soon joined by similar controls over farming with the passage of the Agricultural Adjustment Act (AAA).

Farmers were given subsidies and government-guaranteed price supports, with Washington determining what crops could be grown and what livestock could be raised. Government ordered some crops to be plowed under and some livestock slaughtered, all in the name of centrally planned farm production and pricing.

Much of the urban youth of America were rounded up and sent off to national forests for regimentation and mock military-style drilling as part of the Civilian Conservation Corps (CCC). The Works Progress Administration (WPA) created make-work projects for thousands of able-bodied men, all at taxpayers' expense. Since unemployed artists were "workers" too, they were set to work in government buildings across the land. Even today, in some of the post offices dating from the 1930s, one can see murals depicting happy factory workers and farm hands in a style similar to those produced in Stalin's Russia and Hitler's Germany.

The Constitution of the United States does not give the government the powers of the NIRA, the AAA, the CCC. Or the WPA. Yes, in a democracy, the government would have these powers if the majority or those in power voted them into law. In our Republic however, they clearly exceeded the power we the people gave the Federal government in the Constitution which is the supreme law of the land.

Under the NRA, prices were restricted, that is minimum prices were set and businesses could not sell below those prices. Companies were required to sell their products at a certain price even though they could sell a better product at a price that was lower than the one set by the NRA. Many who refused to sign an NRA declaration adhering to the minimum price were actually jailed. For instance, Sam and Rose Markovitz who owned a dry cleaner business, were jailed because they cleaned a suit for 5 cents less than that demanded by the NRA. Examples are found like this in virtually every business including the tire business, battery business, watch repair business, and investment business. The NRA even had a rule that required when you went to buy a chicken and you reached into the cage to catch the chicken, you had to take the first chicken that touched your hand, and if two chickens than the second and so forth. The Schechter brothers, who sold Kosher chickens in Brooklyn, were taken to court with the accusation they violated this rule.

This was big progressive government dictating prices, wages, and all other aspects of business. A business was forced to place the Blue Eagle in their window to show that they agreed with the tyrannical policies of the NRA and the Roosevelt regime.

Sadly, many people today believe that FDR and his New Deal was the reason for the economic recovery. But in 1937 the United States entered a recession where GDP dropped 10% and unemployment exceeded 20%. The New Deal had many unconstitutional programs and was an economic failure.

FDR built upon the progressive movement begun by Wilson and further eroded our Constitution. The transformation from a republic to a democracy was continued, even enhanced. The government gained more power, it become less and less limited, exceeding the powers we the people wrote into the Constitution, and we the people lost more and more of our liberties.

Jimmy Carter, you remember him, unconstitutionally added the Department of

Education. Upon signing the Department of Education Organization Act Statement in October 1979, Carter said: "Primary responsibility for education should rest with those States, localities, and private institutions that have made our Nation's educational system the best in the world, but the Federal Government has for too long failed to play its own supporting role in education as effectively as it could. Instead of assisting school officials at the local level, it has too often added to their burden. Instead of setting a strong administrative model, the Federal structure has contributed to bureaucratic buck passing. Instead of simulating needed debate of educational issues, the Federal Government has confused its role of junior partner in American education with that of silent partner."

According to the Constitution of the United States, total responsibility for education rests with the States, localities, and private institutions that had made our education system the best in the world. With the unconstitutional control by the federal government, we no longer have an educational system but an indoctrination system. Michele Bachman correctly said, "The Constitution does not specifically enumerate, nor does it give to the federal government the role and duty to superintend over education that historically has been held by the parents and by local communities and by state governments."

Perhaps no single president, not Wilson, not FDR, and certainly not Carter has disregarded and disrespected our Republic and the Constitution of the United States to the extent of Barack Obama. On October 30, 2008, he said, "We are five days from fundamentally transforming the United States." What we learned was that if Obama had completed the statement, it would have read, from a republic with a Constitution that is the supreme law of the land to a true democracy where the majority or those in power have total and complete dictatorial powers over the size and scope of government and over the liberties of the people.

Liberal law professor Garrett Epps stated that, "even for those like me who admire Barack Obama, the constitutional record is disturbingly mixed. Obama leaves the Constitution weaker than at the beginning of his terms." Epps labels Obama's posture to be one of "aggressive compliance," torturing statutory language as far as it can go in order to avoid constitutional claims.

Once Obama lost the congressional majority that allowed him to sign breathtakingly unconstitutional legislation like Obamacare and Dodd-Frank, Obama began using his pen in other ways. Heeding to Woodrow Wilson's progressive view of the administrative state, Obama took out the frustrations of Wilson, FDR, and himself with the checks and balances that inhibited their ability to "fundamentally transform" the country. His administration launched a "We Can't Wait" initiative, with a senior aide explaining that "when Congress won't act, this president will." Obama announced his second-term economic plans, when he said, "I will not allow gridlock, or inaction, or willful indifference to get in our way."

We can only cover a few of Obama's unconstitutional actions. It would take several books to cover them all, so here goes:

Obama believed he had the power to force the secured creditors of Chrysler to accept

30 cents on the dollar. The government has no constitutional authority to make such a demand and the Supreme Court agreed.

Obamacare became law after Chief Justice John Roberts declared that he knew that the law meant tax even though the law that congress approved, and Obama signed said, "individual mandate." Even though Obamacare was then declared to be constitutional, it was not and is not today. Obama proceeded to change the law in several instances with executive authority and not amending the unconstitutional law as would be required by the Constitution. This would include Obama changing how much people were supposed to pay for their own insurance, the timing of when employers of 50 or more people must comply, people were allowed to buy non-complying plans beyond the time allotted by the law, that congressional staff must buy from the exchange, and there are many more.

Obama allowed and encouraged political profiling by the IRS to target conservative organizations such as Tea Party groups.

Obama violated the recess appointment clause to allow appointments to the National Labor Relations Board and the Consumer Financial Protection Bureau.

Through executive order Obama rewrote the immigration law.

Obama denied free speech and due process to those accused of sexual harassment on college campuses.

And Obama's EPA became writer of law, prosecutor, judge, and jury over many matters.

Under the Obama regime, the executive order and regulations became the means of legislating which is in direct contrast to the Constitution which is supposed to be the Supreme Law of the Land. The Obama regime believed they were in a democracy, after all Obama had promised that he would transform the United States into a democracy, where the majority or those in power had no limitations.

Our legislative branch, our executive branch, and our judicial branch of government pay no attention to their constitutional limitations, nor do they pay any attention to the limited powers we the people gave to our government. Our government today believes we are a democracy, and they have no limitations other than the ones, if any, they place on themselves. Congress functions as a national legislature, far beyond its "few and defined" powers, and consistently and constantly encroaches on those reserved to the states and the people.

Examples include education, health care, and various criminal laws.

Even more intrusive are the more than 400 federal agencies that issue thousands of regulations that control every aspect of our lives, from our air and water to our farms and factories. The executive branch now chooses which laws to enforce and which to ignore, and issues its own laws through executive orders and administrative rules.

And the federal courts now routinely decide matters of public policy historically reserved to the states, including life, marriage, and morality. Our federal government today dictates school curriculum, testing, lunch menus, and transgender use of bathrooms and locker rooms; it prohibits mining and burning of coal; it regulates ditches and canals as "waters of the U.S."; it revokes accreditation of colleges whose standards are not "politically correct"; it forces private religious employers to provide contraceptive services; it dictates overtime pay in private employment; it revokes tax-exemptions for nonconforming religious beliefs; it protects wildlife that damages property or threatens domestic livestock; it forces one-size-fits-all health care plans; it limits use of public lands; and on and on.

The administrative state and imperial presidency, so necessary for a democracy and so opposed to a republic, has become a reality in the United States. Unlimited power over the lives of the individual is a reality. The first step in correcting the tyranny of an unlimited government, rule by the majority, democracy, is to recognize the dangers of this unlimited power and the loss of individual freedom and liberty it demands.

CHAPTER 5. **RATIONED LIBERTIES**

Liberties, in a democracy, are at the whim and wish of the majority or those in power.

"It is true that liberty is precious; so precious that it must be carefully rationed." Vladimir Lenin

Liberties in a republic are to be protected and never be under the control of the majority or those in power, but being endowed by the Creator they are inalienable. Personal rights held by an individual which are not bestowed by law, custom, or belief, and which cannot be taken or given away, or transferred to another person, are referred to as "inalienable rights." The U.S. Constitution recognized that certain universal rights cannot be taken away by legislation, because they are beyond the control of a government, being naturally given to every individual at conception, and that these rights are retained throughout life. Natural law does say however, an individual cannot take from another their natural right to life, liberty, and property. If one person takes the life, liberty, or property of another, they have surrendered their rights.

"Liberty is the power to do everything that does not interfere with the rights of others; thus, the exercise of the natural rights of every individual has no limits save those that assure to other members of society the enjoyment of the same rights." Thomas Paine

"He that would make his own liberty secure, must guard even his enemy from oppression; for if he violates this duty, he establishes a precedent that will reach to himself." Thomas Paine

The Declaration of Independence declares, "We hold these truths to be self-evident, that all men are created equal, that they are endowed by their Creator with certain unalienable Rights, that among these are Life, Liberty, and the pursuit of Happiness. That to secure these rights, Governments are instituted among Men, deriving their just powers from the consent of the governed, That whenever any Form of Government becomes destructive of these ends, it is the Right of the People to alter or to abolish it, and to institute new Government ..."

The United States was and is a unique country, We were founded on that belief that our liberties come from God and not from government. The only role government was to ever play in our natural right to life, liberty, and property, or as Thomas Jefferson wrote, our pursuit of happiness, was to protect those natural rights. As we shall see, government was to never limit or abolish any of these rights for the few, for the many, or for all.

It was the writings of John Locke that did much to inspire the American Revolution. Thomas Jefferson ranked Locke as the most important thinker on liberty. Locke helped inspire Thomas Paine's ideas about revolution. Locke influenced George Mason. From Locke, James Madison drew his most fundamental principles of liberty and government. Locke's writings were part of Benjamin Franklin's self-education, and John Adams believed that both girls and boys should learn about Locke.

"Reason, which is that Law," Locke declared, "teaches all Mankind, who would but consult it, that being all equal and independent, no one ought to harm another in his Life, Health, Liberty, or Possessions." Locke envisioned a rule of law as, "have a standing Rule to live by, common to every one of that Society, and made by the Legislative Power erected in it; A Liberty to follow my own Will in all things, where the Rule prescribes not; and not to be subject to the inconstant, uncertain, unknown, Arbitrary Will of another Man."

Locke established that private property is absolutely essential for liberty, "every Man has a Property in his own Person. This no Body has any Right to but himself. The Labour of his Body, and the Work of his Hands, we may say, are properly his." He continues, "The great and chief end therefore, of Men uniting into Commonwealths, and putting themselves under Government, is the Preservation of their Property."

Locke had enormous foresight to see beyond the struggles of his own day, which were directed against monarchy, "Tis a Mistake to think this Fault [tyranny] is proper only to Monarchies; other Forms of Government are liable to it, as well as that. For where-ever the Power that is put in any hands for the Government of the People, and the Preservation of their Properties, is applied to other ends, and used to impoverish, harass, or subdue them to the Arbitrary and Irregular Commands of those that have it: There it presently becomes Tyranny, whether those that thus use it are one or many."

Locke saw forward to the days of democracy, the days when the majority or those in power would harass or subdue and bring about arbitrary law in place of rule of law, tyranny over freedom, and proclaim that liberties are not inalienable but are so precious they must be rationed.

Liberty from the tyranny of government was at the forefront of the call for independence from Great Britain and King George III by the colonists. The colonists believed also that they should be able to be represented if they were to be taxed and thus the call of "No Taxation without Representation." There was also a disagreement as to which law was the law of the land, that passed by the assemblies of the colonists or the declarations of the King. "You Americans have wrong ideas on the Nature of your Constitution," the Earl of Granville told Benjamin Franklin in 1757. "The King in Council is legislator for the Colonies, and when His Majesty's instructions come there, they are the law the land," said the Earl.

There were many laws and declarations imposed on the colonies, including the intolerable acts, as a result of the tea parties conducted throughout the colonies, including the Boston Tea Party on the evening of December 16, 1773. This led to a cry by many that liberty free from the tyranny of government was the only answer. This demand for liberty was proclaimed clearly by Patrick Henry on March 23, 1775, when in Richmond Virginia he stated, "Is life so dear, or peace so sweet, as to be purchased at the price of chains and slavery? Forbid it, Almighty God! I know not what course others may take; but as for me, give me liberty or give me death!"

In January of 1776, "Common Sense" by Thomas Paine was published. It was read far and wide, was discussed where people congregated and changed the minds of many that freedom and liberty were superior to government tyranny. Paine made an eloquent argument that Americans had a unique opportunity to change the course of history by creating a new sort of government in which people were free and had the power to rule themselves.

"We have every opportunity and every encouragement before us, to form the noblest purest constitution on the face of the earth," Paine wrote. "We have it in our power to begin the world over again."

On June 11, 1776, the Continental Congress selected Thomas Jefferson of Virginia, John Adams of Massachusetts, Benjamin Franklin of Pennsylvania, Roger Sherman of Connecticut, and Robert R. Livingston of New York to draft a declaration of independence. Thomas Jefferson was chosen to be the lead writer and is noted as the author of the "Declaration of Independence." It begins thus, "When, in the Course of human Events, it becomes necessary for one People to dissolve the Political Bands which have connected them with another, and to assume, among the Powers of the Earth, the separate and equal Station to which the Laws of Nature and of Nature's God entitle them, a decent Respect to the Opinions of Mankind requires that they should declare the Causes which impel them to the Separation."

This led to a nation that became a republic, purposefully rejecting democracy. This would be a nation where liberty would not be rationed but would be protected from an intruding government determined to limit the liberties of the people when the majority or those in power determined it was in the best interest of government to limit or abolish the liberties of the people.

The US Constitution guarantees a number of rights and liberties to US citizens.

The right to trial by jury in criminal cases is guaranteed. (Article 3, Section 2)

The citizens of each state are entitled to the privileges and immunities of the citizens of every other state. (Article 4, Section 2)

Citizens traveling from state to state are entitled to the same privileges as citizens of the state they are visiting. If a person charged with a crime flees to another state, the governor of the state where the crime was committed can demand the person's return.

The requirement of a Writ of habeas corpus may not be suspended except during invasion or rebellion. (Article 1, Section 9)

In many countries, authorities would take citizens and incarcerate them for months or years without charging them. Those imprisoned had no legal means to protest or challenge the imprisonment. The founding fathers wanted to prohibit this kind of abuse of power in the new United States. Therefore, they included a specific clause in the Constitution to safeguard the right known as habeas corpus. A writ of habeas corpus (which literally means to "produce the body") is a court order demanding that a public official (such as a warden) deliver an imprisoned individual to the court and show a valid reason for that person's detention. Abraham Lincoln violated the right of habeas corpus during the civil war in the case of John Merryman. Lincoln acknowledged that he had violated the Constitution but declared it was necessary to put down the rebellion. The Supreme Court ruled that Lincoln, nor anybody else has the right to suspend this Constitutional Right.

People arrested for being in Washington D.C. on January 6, 2021, have been denied habeas corpus, some have been jailed without being charged with a crime, they have been denied the right to bail, many have been placed in solitary confinement, and some were held indefinitely without appearing in court or being given a court date. These American Citizens were denied their Constitutional rights by the United States Government.

Neither Congress nor the states can pass a bill of attainder. (Article 1, Section 9)

A Bill of Attainder is a legislative act that punishes a specific individual or group without a trial or judicial hearing. Nathan Hale would be a reason why this was a protection written into our Constitution. Nathan Hale was captured on September 21, 1776, by the British while attempting to return to his regiment, having penetrated the British lines on Long Island to gather information. He was hanged without trial the next day.

Neither Congress nor the states can pass ex-post facto laws. (Article 1, Section 9)

An ex-post facto law would be passing a law that retroactively alters a defendant's rights, especially by criminalizing and imposing punishment for an act that was not criminal or punishable at the time it was committed, or by increasing the severity of a crime from its level at the time the crime was committed, or by increasing the punishment for a crime from the punishment imposed at the time the crime was committed, or by taking away from the protections afforded the defendant by the law as it existed when the act was committed.

No law impairing the obligation of contracts may be passed by states. (Article 1, Section 10)

This was intended to prohibit the states from interfering with private contracts.

No religious test or qualification for holding federal office is allowed. (Article 6) ...but no religious Test shall ever be required as a Qualification to any Office or public Trust under the United States.

Religious tests are becoming more and more common in Senate hearings for people nominated to serve. Some examples would be when several Democratic members of the judiciary committee questioned whether Amy Coney Barrett's faith, she's a Roman Catholic, would keep her from following the law. Bernie Sanders asked a nominee about an article he wrote in support of his religion and his belief that Jesus is the true God. When the nominee answered in the affirmative, Sanders stated that he was not fit for service.

The religious test is being applied more and more frequently, not only in the Senate, but it is becoming more and more common as a qualification for hiring of federal employees.

No titles of nobility would be allowed. (Article 1, Section 9)

In addition to these liberties, other specific liberties are protected in the Bill of Rights.

Interestingly, a bill of rights had scarcely been discussed during the Constitutional

Convention. George Mason mentioned it in the last days of the Convention, but almost as an afterthought. When brought to a vote, every state voted against it. The consensus was that the Constitution should be concerned with "objects of a general nature" and that the preservation of individual rights should be left to the states. Jefferson, who was not a delegate to the Convention but was serving as United States Minister to France, gave a qualified approval to the Constitution but noted the absence of a bill of rights. He said, "A bill of rights is what the people are entitled to against every government on earth, general or particular, and what on just government should refuse, or rest on inference."

The absence of a "bill of rights" turned out to be a major obstacle to the Constitution's ratification by the states. It would take four more years of intense debate before the new government's form would be resolved. Those who opposed including a bill of rights did so on the ground that it was unnecessary. They also argued that it would be dangerous because any listing of rights could potentially be interpreted as exhaustive and that any rights omitted could be considered as not retained.

Those who argued for a bill of rights were afraid of a strong centralized government and refused to support the Constitution without a bill of rights. This faction argued that in a state of nature people were entirely free. In society some rights were yielded for the common good. But there were some rights so fundamental that to give them up would be contrary to the common good. These rights, which should always be retained by the people, needed to be explicitly stated in a bill of rights that would clearly define the limits of government. A bill of rights would also, they argued, serve as a fire bell for the people, enabling them to immediately know when their rights were threatened.

James Madison, who had originally opposed a bill of rights, understood that ratification of the Constitution could only happen if a promise to include a bill of rights was made. Madison told Jefferson that although he never really opposed a bill of rights, he now favored it because it is so anxiously desired by others. He also later agreed that a bill of rights would serve as an additional guard in favor of liberty. It was this sentiment that prevailed.

Recently freed from the despotic English monarchy, the American people wanted strong guarantees that the new government would not trample upon their newly won freedoms of speech, press, and religion, nor upon their right to be free from warrantless searches and seizures. The American Bill of Rights, inspired by Jefferson and drafted by James Madison, was adopted, and by December 15, 1791, three-fourths of the states had ratified the Bill of Rights. The Constitution's first ten amendments, known as the Bill of Rights, became a part of the United States Constitution and thus the supreme law of the land.

The Bill of Rights:

Preamble

Congress of the United States begun and held at the City of New-York, on Wednesday the fourth of March, one thousand seven hundred and eighty-nine.

THE Conventions of a number of the States, having at the time of their adopting the Constitution, expressed a desire, in order to prevent misconstruction or abuse of its powers, that further declaratory and restrictive clauses should be added: And as extending the ground of public confidence in the Government, will best ensure the beneficent ends of its institution.

RESOLVED by the Senate and House of Representatives of the United States of America, in Congress assembled, two thirds of both Houses concurring, that the following Articles be proposed to the Legislatures of the several States, as amendments to the Constitution of the United States, all, or any of which Articles, when ratified by three fourths of the said Legislatures, to be valid to all intents and purposes, as part of the said Constitution: viz.

First Amendment

Congress shall make no law respecting an establishment of religion, or prohibiting the free exercise thereof; or abridging the freedom of speech, or of the press, or the right of the people peaceably to assemble, and to petition the Government for a redress of grievances.

Second Amendment

A well-regulated Militia, being necessary to the security of a free State, the right of the people to keep and bear Arms, shall not be infringed.

Third Amendment

No Soldier shall, in time of peace be quartered in any house, without the consent of the Owner; nor in time of war, but in a manner to be prescribed by law.

Fourth Amendment

The right of the people to be secure in their persons, houses, papers, and effects, against unreasonable searches and seizures, shall not be violated, and no Warrants shall issue, but upon probable cause, supported by Oath or affirmation, and particularly describing the place to be searched, and the persons or things to be seized.

Fifth Amendment

No person shall be held to answer for a capital, or otherwise infamous crime, unless on a presentment or indictment of a Grand Jury, except in cases arising in the land or naval forces, or in the Militia, when in actual service in time of War or public danger; nor shall any person be subject for the same offence to be twice put in jeopardy of life or limb; nor shall be compelled in any criminal case to be a witness against himself; nor be deprived of life, liberty, or property, without due process of law; nor shall private property be taken for public use without just compensation.

Sixth Amendment

In all criminal prosecutions, the accused shall enjoy the right to a speedy and public trial, by an impartial jury of the State and district wherein the crime shall have been committed; which district shall have been previously ascertained by law, and to be informed of the nature and cause of the accusation; to be confronted with the witnesses against him; to have compulsory process for obtaining witnesses in his favor; and to have the assistance of counsel for his defense.

Seventh Amendment

In Suits at common law, where the value in controversy shall exceed twenty dollars, the right of trial by jury shall be preserved, and no fact tried by a jury shall be otherwise reexamined in any Court of the United States, then according to the rules of common law.

Eighth Amendment

Excessive bail shall not be required, nor excessive fines imposed, nor cruel and unusual punishments inflicted.

Ninth Amendment

The enumeration in the Constitution of certain rights shall not be construed to deny or disparage others retained by the people.

Tenth Amendment

The powers not delegated to the United States by the Constitution, nor prohibited by it to the States, are reserved to the States respectively, or to the people.

ARTICLES in addition to, and Amendment of the Constitution of the United States of America, proposed by Congress, and ratified by the Legislatures of the several States, pursuant to the fifth Article of the original Constitution.

We will be discussing these amendments and how they complement the Declaration of Independence which acknowledges that our rights and liberties come from our Creator and not from government.

The First Amendment is very specific. It states congress shall make no law respecting an establishment of religion, or prohibiting the free exercise thereof. The establishment of religion was prohibited because there were colonies with state sponsored religions. In England, the Church of England was a state sponsored religion. All who paid taxes to the English government, supported the Church of England even if they were not members or did not attend it. In the colonies, 5 colonies sponsored the Church of England, 3 colonies sponsored the Congregational Church, and 5 colonies sponsored no church. The Constitution prohibits the United States government from sponsoring any religion, even secularism or atheism.

The First Amendment also says congress can make no law prohibiting the free exercise of religion. Because congress is the only branch of government with the right to legislate, there can be no laws prohibiting for instance prayer, Bible reading, or religious discussions, even on public property. We know this because church services were held in the Capitol until well after the Civil War. The courts are violating the Constitution when they prohibit the practice of religion on public grounds. Only an amendment to the First Amendment would constitutionally enable the prohibition of the practice of religion like prayer, Bible reading, or religious discussions in public or private places. The majority or those in power are violating the constitution by restricting the free practice thereof, they are acting as they could in a democracy.

The First Amendment goes on to say that congress can make no law abridging the freedom of speech, or of the press, or the right of the people peaceably to assemble, and to petition the Government for a redress of grievances. To abridge would mean to reduce in scope. To abridge or reduce in scope any of the above liberties would require an amendment to the First Amendment defining the exact area of abridgement. We have all heard the line by Justice Holmes that one cannot holler fire in a crowded theater, and many now consider this to be the law. (In the case where Holmes made this statement, the case was not about a fire, nor did it have anything to do with a theater. It was simply an analogy.) It is not and cannot be the law. It cannot be the law because the First Amendment prohibits it from being the law, it is an abridgement of free speech, and the courts cannot make law or override the Constitution.

 Few would argue that to "holler fire in a crowded theater" would be a wise practice. Few would argue that anybody who would purposefully endanger others in this manner should not suffer the consequences for any damages their dangerous and foolish action caused. We were founded as a republic, and in our republic the power of the government is limited, and the liberties of the people are unlimited. With unlimited liberties comes tremendous responsibilities. The founders understood that freedom and self-government absolutely depended on the practice of virtue. John Adams wrote, "the only foundation of a free Constitution is pure virtue."

Congress can make no law abridging. This also applies to the freedom of the press. A free press must be responsible, even though for most of our history it has not. The press was so vicious and one sided during the campaign of 1828, Mrs. Andrew Jackson is believed to have died because of the attacks of the press upon her. She died before her husband's inauguration.

Abridging applies to peaceably assembling. In today's world a political faction has redefined peaceably to include riots, arson, looting, assault, and even murder. The purpose of that faction in protecting those who have moved beyond peaceably, is to promote their agenda. This faction, which has become a threat to our republic, believe that any means is acceptable so long as it advances their cause to transform the United States from a republic to a democracy. Just as in the case of free speech, those who would harm the person or property of others, must be held responsible for that harm.

We do have the right to make a complaint against our government and not be afraid of punishment or reprisals. This liberty seems to be abused more by local governments and school boards than by the federal government. A republic, and our liberties, require a responsible and virtuous citizenry who are certain to elect virtuous people to represent them.

No law prohibiting and no law abridging is absolute. In a republic, the liberties of the people are absolute. In a democracy, liberties are whatever the majority or those in power determine them to be, liberties are subject to any restrictions placed upon them by that majority or those in power, even to being abolished if that is what the majority or those in power determine.

The Second Amendment is also definite. The right of the people to keep and bear arms shall not be infringed. There are no qualifications as to whether these arms are assault arms or arms of war. The second amendment does not equivocate. The reasons for this amendment and its intent are quite clear, they are for self-protection and for protection against an aspiring tyrannical government.

"The supposed quietude of a good man allures the ruffian; while on the other hand, arms like laws discourage and keep the invader and plunderer in awe, and preserve order in the world as well as property. The same balance would be preserved were all the world destitute of arms, for all would be alike; but since some will not, others dare not lay them aside... Horrid mischief would ensue were one half the world deprived of the use of them." Thomas Paine

"Before a standing army can rule, the people must be disarmed as they are in almost every kingdom of Europe. The supreme power in America cannot enforce unjust laws by the sword; because the whole body of the people are armed, and constitute a force superior to any band of regular troops that can be, on any pretense, raised in the United States." Noah Webster

The Third Amendment says no soldier shall, in time of peace be quartered in any house, without the consent of the owner; nor in time of war, but in a manner to be prescribed by law.

This amendment was critical to early Americans. The British had forced colonists to give British soldiers meals and places to sleep. It was a point of great contention. It is hard to imagine this amendment would ever be applicable again, however, in a democracy we can never be sure.

The Fourth Amendment is being violated more and more. It specifically says the right of the citizen to be protected against unreasonable searches and seizures, shall not be violated, and no Warrants shall issue without probable cause.

TSA searches your bags with no Warrant and no probable cause. Drones fly overhead and collect data without a Warrant and no probable cause. Department of Homeland Security keeps records on phone data and other types of communications. Different law enforcement agencies including the DOJ, the FBI, the CIA, and local law enforcement agencies completely ignore the fourth amendment. More and more it is being abused for political reasons. An example would be the John Doe raids in Wisconsin when on October 3, 2013, some Wisconsin conservatives had their homes and offices raided in a politically motivated investigation.

In the early morning darkness, law enforcement officers swept into sleeping middle class neighborhoods in several coordinated, multi-county raids. They forcibly entered homes and offices with wide-open warrants and spent the next several hours rooting through the possessions of not only the conservatives they were targeting, but those of their spouses and children. They carried out boxes of files, personal planners, and electronic devices. And they told the residents of the homes they invaded, that if these conservatives, even their kids, said anything to anyone about what happened there, they could go to jail.

This is the activity that is outlawed in a republic, but is acceptable in a democracy so long as the majority or those in power approve it.

The Fifth Amendment most famously says that a person does not have to testify against himself. But it also states that a person must be indicted by a grand jury, cannot be tried twice for the same crime, and cannot be deprived of life, liberty, or property, without due process of law; nor shall private property be taken for public use without just compensation.

January 6th, 2021, defendants were arrested and held without being indicted, they were placed in prison and denied any semblance of due process.

Defendants who have been acquitted in a state court have been tried again in federal court for the same crime. In 1992, four Los Angeles police officers were acquitted for the beating of Rodney King. All four men were acquitted in state court. However, two of the men were subsequently tried and convicted in federal court for the same crime.

The Department of Justice announced a federal policy that allows local and state police to seize cash and property from those who are suspected of crimes, even if criminal charges have not been filed.

The Fifth Amendment is a prime example of how republics and democracies differ. Under a republic the unconstitutional changes that have been made to the fifth amendment should have been done by amending the Constitution. Under a democracy the majority or those in power could have just proclaimed these changes, which is what happened.

The Sixth Amendment says that In all criminal prosecutions, the accused shall enjoy the right to a speedy trial, and to be informed of the nature and cause of the accusation.

More and more we are forsaking this important liberty for political purposes. This is again shown in the Jan 6th trials. The political faction calling for our republic to be transformed into a democracy has had people arrested, and held in solitary confinement. These people have no court date or charges made. These individuals being unconstitutionally held, are now political prisoners. One of the reasons for this amendment was to prevent our nation from going down that road of democracy where political prisoners are common. Like these other nine amendments, the Sixth Amendment was created to limit the power of government.

The Seventh Amendment says in suits at common law, where the value in controversy shall exceed twenty dollars, the rights to a jury trial is preserved.

This amendment should perhaps be amended to raise twenty dollars to an amount more reflective of values today.

The Eighth Amendment says that excessive bail shall not be required, nor excessive fines imposed, nor cruel and unusual punishments inflicted.

This amendment is subjective. More than excessive bail or fines being required or imposed, we are in a time where subjective bail is required, and subjective fines are imposed for political motivation. Those sympathetic to the transformation movement from a republic to a democracy are treated more favorably than those who oppose the transformation. This is not acceptable under a republic but is exactly how a democracy operates. We will discuss this concept more in the chapter about "rule of law."

The Ninth Amendment says the enumeration in the Constitution of certain rights shall not be construed to deny or disparage others retained by the people.

This amendment is very important but seldom mentioned. It is important to understand the meaning and purpose.

The faction who contended that a bill of rights was unnecessary, responded to those opposing ratification of the Constitution because of the lack of a declaration of fundamental rights by arguing that, inasmuch as it would be impossible to list all rights, it would be dangerous to list some and thereby lend support to the argument that government was unrestrained as to those rights not listed. Madison responded to this argument when he presented his proposed amendments to the House of

Representatives. "It has been objected also against a bill of rights, that, by enumerating particular exceptions to the grant of power, it would disparage those rights which were not placed in that enumeration; and it might follow by implication, that those rights which were not singled out, were intended to be assigned into the hands of the General Government, and were consequently insecure. This is one of the most plausible arguments I have ever heard against the admission of a bill of rights into this system; but I conceive, that it may be guarded against. I have attempted it, as gentlemen may see by turning to the last clause of the fourth resolution." It is clear from its text and from Madison's statement that the Amendment states but a rule of construction, making clear that a Bill of Rights might not by implication be taken to increase the powers of the national government in areas not enumerated, and that it does not contain within itself any guarantee of a right or a proscription of an infringement. The liberties and rights of the citizens of the United States were to be unlimited and could not be infringed, abridged, or limited, even those which are not stated in the Constitution or the Bill of Rights. Never in our republic were rights and liberties to be rationed, as called for by Lenin and done so in a democracy.

The Tenth Amendment says that he powers not delegated to the United States by the Constitution, nor prohibited by it to the States, are reserved to the States respectively, or to the people.

In Article 1 and Section 8 of the United States Constitution, the founders specifically listed the powers that we the people were giving to the federal government. The Tenth Amendment is clear that any power not specifically listed in Article 1 and Section 8 of the Constitution is off limits to the federal government and is under the authority of the States and or the people.

In a republic the power of government is limited. That is exactly what the Tenth Amendment reinforces. In a democracy the power of government is whatever the majority or those in power say it is. Thomas Jefferson told us that the Tenth Amendment is the foundation of our Constitution.

If you have learned nothing else in this chapter, it is important that you understand that in a republic, the government does not have the authority to infringe, abridge, limit, or abolish the rights and liberties of the people, even if the majority or those in power determine it is in the best interest of government to do so. The majority or those in power are restricted from limiting the rights and liberties of the minority, even if the minority is considered to be a political enemy of the majority or those in power. In a democracy the majority or those in power define what the liberties and rights of the people are. The majority or those in power can and do, in a democracy, follow the teachings of Lenin that liberties are so precious they must be rationed.

CHAPTER 6. **RULE OF LAW OR ARBITRARY LAW**

"Justice is indiscriminately due to all, without regard to numbers, wealth, or rank." John Jay, First Chief Justice of the Supreme Court

"There can be no truer principle than this, that every individual of the community at large has an equal right to the protection of government." Alexander Hamilton

More than two hundred and thirty years ago, our Founders created and signed the Constitution of the United States. This written constitution established that the United States of America would be a nation governed by the rule of law. The concepts embodied in the phrase "rule of law" are simple. Its simplicity derives from the fact that the underlying notion is clear: all persons, regardless of race, ethnicity, gender, religion, sexual orientation, economic status, social status, political affiliation, or other group or individual characteristics, are equal in the eyes of the law.

A critical factor of rule of law is to be sure that the judges presiding over disputes are independent, impartial, and well-qualified. The notion of "impartiality" implies that judges do not have preconceptions about the matter put before them, and that they must not act in ways that promote the interests of one of the parties or a political agenda. If we are to remain a nation committed to rule of law, it is essential we resist attempts by political and special interest groups to politicize the judicial branch and transform our judges to nothing more than "politicians in robes." The third branch of government was not conceived as being, and must not be, a political branch of government. Our judges must remain free to make their rulings based on facts and applicable law, and never to further one partisan, special interest, or political point of view. Our Founders envisioned and intended a judicial system separate from the political branches of government; a system designed to fulfill the promise that this country would provide a government based on the rule of law. We all are responsible for ensuring the continued viability of that vision.

For rule of law to exist it is essential that there be an open and transparent system of making laws, and that laws are applied predictably and uniformly. Openness and transparency are essential. If people are unable to know and understand what the law is, they cannot be expected to follow it. At the same time, people deserve to know why a particular law has been passed and why they are being asked to obey it.

The rule of law also requires that people can expect predictable results from the legal system; the laws must not be applied arbitrarily. Predictable results means that people who act in the same way can expect the law to treat them in the same way. If similar actions do not produce similar legal outcomes, people cannot use the law to guide their actions, and rule of law does not exist.

A society based on rule of law and practicing rule of law is essential for a free society. A republic must be based on rule of law and rule of law must be practiced; that is the law must be easily understood, it must be readily available to all, the law must be applied equally to all, the outcome must be predictable, and courts must not allow any personal prejudices to interfere in administering the law.

The term arbitrary describes a course of action or a decision that is not based on reason or judgment, but it is based on personal will or discretion without regard to rules or standards. Therefore, arbitrary law would be a ruling or decision that is not necessarily based on the law, but it is based on the personal will, discretion, or prejudices of those having authority over the case.

John Locke stated, "Freedom of men under government is to have a standing rule to live by, common to every one of that society and made by the legislative power vested in it and not to be subject to the inconstant, uncertain, arbitrary will of another man."

Locke went on to say that tyranny is the result of arbitrary law when he stated, "For where-ever the Power that is put in any hands for the Government of the People, and the Preservation of their Properties, is applied to other ends, and made use of too impoverish, harass, or subdue them to the Arbitrary and Irregular Commands of those that have it: There it presently becomes Tyranny, whether those that thus use it are one or many."

As an example, the English King possessed arbitrary power, meaning that his power was not confined by an external source of law because he was the law. This means that if the King one day decided that a Queen who could not produce a son had no value and therefore must be eliminated, the Queen could be eliminated, and no one could argue otherwise. The Kings actions were up to his will and discretion. The King was not confined by any external law.

In the days of the Roman Empire, it was attempted to bring some predictability to their legal system, but there were different systems for people of different status. Rome also continued to allow arbitrary decisions by officials. In the Roman system, the penalty for a given crime depended on your citizenship status and your social class. In general, punishments for the senatorial and equestrian orders were milder than those for the ordinary citizen. Also, punishment for a citizen would be less severe than for a noncitizen for the same crime.

In the provinces, legal matters were under the control of the governor. In criminal cases, the governor had sole authority, and he had no limitations on how he treated noncitizens. A provincial governor was not limited by the statutory offenses governing the courts in Rome, he could try on any pretext and inflict any penalty he wanted to maintain order in his province.

The governor determined the law. They had no restraints. This is tyranny. As we look at history we learn that Kings, Queens, Czars, and Emperors also had unrestrained power.

Where the law can be applied without restraint, without predictability, without being published for all to know, without being understandable, applied differently to different people for different reasons, tyranny is the result. Where an individual, an oligarchy, those in power, or even the majority can apply the law to different people for different reasons, the system of law is arbitrary and not based on rule of law.

John Locke told us, "the difference betwixt a king and a tyrant to consist only in this, that one makes the laws the bounds of his power, and the good of the public, the end of his government; the other makes all give way to his own will and appetite."

Where anybody, be it a king, a tyrant, a president, a congressman, committee, a governor, a mayor, or any official, would go beyond the bounds of their power, or would apply the law in an arbitrary way, for their own will and appetite, they have employed arbitrary power and have assumed the role of a tyrant.

This would be the case in the governors of Rome, many of the tyrannical Emperors of Rome such as Caligula, Czars of Russia such as Ivan IV, notorious dictators such as Genghis Kahn, Lenin, Stalin, Hitler, Mao, Kim Jong Il, Pol Pot, Idi Amin, and many others throughout the years. These individuals contrived, declared, or manipulated the law to fit their needs and wishes. Many times, they applied arbitrary law out of spite and for political purposes.

Joseph Stalin is well known for his use of arbitrary law. The law was what he said it would be and the outcome of the trial ended the way he orchestrated it. Ironically, when Stalin introduced his new constitution, he was also engineering the arrest of thousands of Communist Party and government officials who for his own reasons considered these officials as threats to his political power. Most of those arrested were tried in secret or received no trial at all. A small minority of well-known Soviet officials did receive highly publicized public trials in Moscow between 1936 and 1938. Often based on forced confessions, the trials made a mockery of the idea of due process of law and rule of law. All the participants of these so-called "show trials," including the judges, served Stalin's political evil.

Under Hitler, Germany became a police state characterized by arbitrary arrest and imprisonment of political and ideological opponents in concentration camps. "Protective custody" was redefined in 1933 so police power became independent of judicial controls. In Nazi terminology, protective custody came to mean arrest, without judicial review, of real and potential opponents of the regime. Hitler established special courts throughout Germany to try politically sensitive cases and assure the "proper" verdict.

According to Human Rights Watch, North Korean authorities arbitrarily arrest, unfairly prosecute, and severely mistreat people for conducting private business activity, with punishments varying with bribes and connections. Human Rights Watch interviewed 12 North Koreans involved in private commerce who had fled to South Korea. Those interviewed said that when authorities confronted them about engaging in business activities, their fate depended on their capacity to pay bribes or mobilize personal connections, or the government's need for forced labor.

These are characteristic of arbitrary law which would be a ruling or decision that is not necessarily based on the law, but it is based on the personal will, discretion, or prejudices of those having authority over the case. There was not a standing rule by which to live, a rule common to every one of that society and made by the legislative power vested in it and not subject to the inconstant, uncertain, arbitrary will of another man.

In a free society, it is essential that rule of law prevail. This is a distinguishing difference between a republic and a democracy. The more a society is transformed into democracy, the more prevalent arbitrary law becomes. As the majority or those in power become bolder and ignore the law to implement their agenda or enhance their power, they prosecute their political enemies under their proclaimed law, and ignore the law when it applies to their political allies. In the examples we have used to show where arbitrary law prevailed, they were cases where the tyrannical element prosecuted to punish their political enemies.

In the last several decades in the United States, a time when the transformation from a republic to a democracy has progressed to where our nation resembles a democracy much more than a republic, we are witnessing both; prosecution of political enemies and protection of political allies.

In 1894, a group of unemployed workers led by Jacob Coxey, the group became known as Coxey's Army, marched on Washington D.C. to bring attention to the plight of the worker in the economic downturn of that time. Coxey rose to speak to the group on the Capitol grounds but was arrested before he completed the first two paragraphs of his speech. The crime for which he was arrested, walking on the grass.

Federal authorities arrested Joseph Tigano III in 2008 and charged him with running a marijuana-growing operation. Tigano entered a plea of not guilty and insisted that his case move quickly to trial. Instead, he was kept in jail for nearly seven years before he finally appeared before a jury. During his nearly seven-year pretrial incarceration, Tigano loudly and repeatedly invoked his Sixth Amendment right to a speedy trial. Because Tigano kept bringing up the Sixth Amendment, he was forced to undergo three separate court-ordered examinations to determine whether he was competent to be tried. According to one of the prosecutors involved in the case, "Mr. Tigano III had been sort of demanding his speedy trial, which is part of the prompting for the Court sending him out for this evaluation." Tigano passed all three exams with flying colors.

Arbitrary law now holds political prisoners in solitary confinement in Washington D.C. jails. There "are about 50, plus or minus, individuals that have been detained and have been in prison for months, and will likely remain in prison for many more months until their day in court, if and when that comes. A political faction claimed that their political enemies committed an insurgency on January 6, 2021. Not one of the people arrested had been charged with insurgency. Most were charged with misdemeanors, like trespassing, reminiscent of Jacob Coxey.

Bail has been denied to these people on the pretense that they are flight risks, or a threat to the public.

The conditions in the D.C. jail in particular are getting to a point of not only being unconstitutional, but violating every single basic human right. "They are getting to a point where people have to speak out, and they have to know about what's going on," one individual said, adding that prisoners are being instilled with a "level of fear."

"They are being retaliated against for various different reasons. ... Anything that they do, or if anybody speaks up on their behalf, all of a sudden they get targeted even further and then get put into a dangerous, unsanitary condition," the same individual said.

This is in contrast to Elizabeth Duke, who was charged with several counts related to domestic terrorism for her involvement in the 1983 Capitol Hill bombing, and was released on bail. Duke did flee and remains a fugitive despite former U.S. Attorney General Eric Holder asking a federal magistrate to "kill" her outstanding arrest warrant in 2009.

Portland, Oregon was a city under siege in the summer of 2020. Rioting, looting, arson, and assault were occurring under the name of peacefully protesting. Many supporters of the rioters also referred to the uprising as a peaceful protest. There were some arrests, but roughly 90% of Portland rioters who were arrested in the month of September had charges dropped by the Multnomah County District Attorney's Office. Interfering with a peace officer, disorderly conduct and rioting charges were abandoned in a group of 213 arrests by Oregon State Police.

"Most suspects have had their charges dropped or dismissed, some as soon as the day after their arrest," it was reported. "As of October 5, charges had been dropped in around 90% of the cases stemming from September's protest activity." This despite laws being unquestionably broken.

Hillary Clinton used a private email server for government work as Secretary of State and then proceeded to delete thousands of those emails. Over the course of an investigation, FBI agents found thousands of emails that contained information that should have been treated as government secrets, FBI Director James Comey stated, including eight messages that had Top Secret information in them. All those messages had been sent or received through unsecure, unclassified channels on Clinton's private e-mail network. And while agents found no direct evidence that the network was hacked, the FBI said it is possible some "hostile actors" may have done so.

The law governing this action is quite specific. The laws regarding handling of classified information do not authorize punishing government officials for carelessness, but for what is termed "gross negligence". One section of the Espionage Act, 18USC793(f), says anyone authorized to handle secrets who "through gross negligence permits the same to be removed from its proper place of custody ... shall be fined under this title or imprisoned not more than ten years, or both."

Hillary Clinton was a candidate for President of the United States at the time this investigation was being conducted. In a dramatic statement that had a direct impact on the presidential campaign, FBI Director James Comey said Hillary Clinton and her aides may have violated the law in using a private email server when she was Secretary of State, but that their actions didn't warrant criminal charges. In its year-long investigation of how government secrets got onto the server, Comey said, the FBI found "evidence of potential violations of the statutes regarding the handling of classified information," but he said, "we are expressing to Justice our view that no charges are appropriate in this case."

Comey concluded the use of the private email server was against the law and the violation was augmented because of government secrets. Comey ignored the "gross negligence" statement in the law, and in fact rewrote the law to fit his needs and remove Clinton from facing a grand jury for her crime and further investigation because he said she had no willful intent. This is democracy

During testimony before the Senate Intelligence Committee, then fired FBI Director James Comey said he leaked his memo of an Oval Office meeting with the President to the press, claiming it was "recollection" of his conversation "as a private citizen." He then admitted to the committee that he gave it to "a friend" to give to a reporter, hoping it would "prompt the appointment of a special prosecutor."

During this same hearing, Comey explained that as FBI Director, he had investigated others for leaking information to the press.

No investigation was taken, no charges or arrests were made. The matter was ignored. To investigate was not in the best interest of the majority or those in power. This is democracy.

Former FBI Deputy Director Andrew McCabe was fired in 2018 after the inspector general of the Department of Justice concluded McCabe had leaked classified information and lied to bureau agents. The government has subsequently agreed to expunge McCabe's record and restore his pension, including $200,000 the government said it owed him. To act against McCabe would not have been in the best interest of the majority or those in power. This is democracy.

Those who advocate for democracy, those who believe the majority or those in power make the law, enforce the law, and adjudicate the law, those who believe in arbitrary law, also understand the necessity of intimidation for them to remain in power.

All men have the potential to be tyrants. As Aristotle warned . . .

"The three aims of the tyrant are, one, the humiliation of his subjects; he knows that a humiliated man will not conspire against anybody; two, the creation of mistrust among them; for a tyrant is not to be overthrown until men begin to have confidence in one another — and this is the reason why tyrants are at war with the good; they are under the idea that their power is endangered by them, not only because they will not be ruled despotically, but also because they are too loyal to one another and to other men, and do not inform against one another or against other men — three, the tyrant desires that all his subjects shall be incapable of action, for no one attempts what is impossible and they will not attempt to overthrow a tyrant if they are powerless."

Lenin understood the necessity of using force as intimidation. The FBI has become the American Cheka as the transformation from republic to democracy is being conducted. Lenin emphasized the high esteem in which he held the Cheka. He highly praised their work. "The important thing for us is that the Extraordinary Commissions are directly exercising the dictatorship of the proletariat, and in that respect their services are inestimable. There is no way of liberating the masses except by forcibly suppressing the exploiters. That is what the Extraordinary Commissions are doing, and therein lies their service to the proletariat."

The ends justify the means is the rule of democracy. The majority or those in power define the means to bring about their ultimate ends. We see how the FBI is emulating the Cheka in their methods of intimidating. Examples are the Cheka like FBI raids on the homes of Paul Manafort and Roger Stone.

Manafort and his wife were asleep at 6 a.m. when a dozen fully armed FBI agents stormed Manafort's Virginia home. In view of Manafort's prior cooperation with law enforcement, the paramilitary raid clearly was overkill and intimidation was the only purpose.

It is likely that the raid occurred because Manafort had not "flipped" by revealing damning evidence about other witnesses. Manafort was sentenced to more than seven years in prison and placed in solitary confinement for months because he was deemed guilty of being an enemy of the state.

Arbitrary law was exhibited again in this case as Tony Podesta, brother of Hillary Clinton's campaign manager, John Podesta, was given immunity for the same crimes for which Manafort was charged.

Roger Stone received the Cheka treatment at his Florida home. Stone was quoted as saying that 29 FBI agents "pounded on the door" when he was in his pajamas, pointed automatic weapons at him, and "terrorized" his wife and dogs.

"It was absolutely ridiculous," said ex-FBI agent Peter Yachmetz. "They were trying to get a point across, and it was leaked to CNN. It was inappropriate and improper," Yachmetz added. "I cannot recall banging on anyone's door at 6 a.m. for a white-collar crime."

This "double standard" has been consistent in collectivist takeovers or transformations of a republic to a democracy. It is the goal of the collectivist to silence opponents and intimidate the population so they will conform to the dictates of the government. "Double standard" is indeed a euphemism for arbitrary law. It is arbitrary law when different standards are applied to different people for political purposes or any other purposes.

That is the definition of arbitrary law; the law is applied in such a way as to arrive at the desired results of those applying the law. Arbitrary law is the standard in a democracy. As the democracy becomes more and more dictatorial, the application of the law becomes more and more arbitrary.

Rule of law must prevail in a republic. The law must be applied fairly and equally. Factors such as political affiliation can never be considered. The use of the law for the purpose of intimidation must never occur.

The more a nation transforms from a republic to a democracy, the more the law will be applied arbitrarily and the more the law will be used for the purpose of intimidation. As you observe a society, the more you hear "double standard" when the application of the law is discussed, beware, because that society is becoming more and more of a democracy and moving closer and closer to a tyrannical dictatorship.

CHAPTER 7. **DOES IT MATTER**

Republic or Democracy, Does it Matter? The differences are real, as we have discussed. The founders understood the differences and consciously and overwhelmingly chose republic over democracy. Americans today have little to no idea as to what those differences are and why they matter. They are not being taught the differences in school and many people who write on these differences are products of those institutions who do not know, or fail to teach those differences.

Here is an explanation of what is thought to be the differences. You should by now be able to understand how wrong the following explanation is.

Difference Between Democracy and Republic by Surbhi S,

"There are many forms of political systems which are prevalent in different countries of the world for a long time like monarchy, oligarchy, anarchy, democracy, and republic. Of these forms of government, democracy and a republic are quite often juxtaposed, but there is a fine line amidst the two.

Democracy refers to the system of masses, i.e., a political system dominated by citizens of the country. Under this system, the general public possess a certain degree of power and authority and takes part in the decision-making process of the state.

Republic refers to the state wherein the ultimate power lies in the hands of the people and their elected representatives. Here, the representatives are chosen by the people to vote on behalf of them."

What Surbhi S described would be the differences between a direct democracy and a representative democracy. This is very common and is becoming a common refrain when supposedly knowledgeable Americans are asked to explain the differences.

Joe Biden insists, "the United States is committed to strengthening our democracy." Nancy Pelosi commands the nation to serve as, "a symbol of democracy to the world." Chuck Schumer calls for, "systemic democracy reforms . . . to save our democracy." Bernie Sanders harangues, "democracy must win." Alexandria Ocasio-Cortez perceives a "very real risk" that democracy will disappear.

Unfortunately, it is not only those on the far left that want to save our democracy. Jim Banks (R-IN) has introduced a piece of legislation called the Save Democracy Act.

"We are really the only significant experiment in democracy, and preserving liberal democracy is an extraordinary challenge," Mitt Romney said.

Susan Collins has stated, "The right to vote is the hallmark of a democracy. It is what distinguishes us from authoritarian regimes where elections are tainted -- if they are held at all -- where the free and fair elections that define America do not exist."

John McCain said that Russian hacking during the 2016 election threatens to "destroy democracy."

And the list goes on and on. Listen to pundits, read opinion editorials, read journalists, listen to opinion programs, and listen to politicians, office holders, and bureaucrats, and count the times they refer to the United States as a democracy. The times they claim they are fighting for democracy; it dwarfs the number of times you will hear republic. **Does this matter?**

Words have taken on different meanings over the years. It changes how the words are used. Egregious was used to describe something that was not common or ordinary. So, if you were distinguished or eminent, you could be egregious, such as being an egregious doctor. Now egregious behavior is more likely to be considered offensive and unnecessary.

Senile was originally used to describe old people in general, but it changed over time to describe someone who has lost some (or all) of their mental faculties with age.

Although naughty is used to describe children (or adults) who misbehave, that wasn't always the case. Naughty was used to describe a child too young to speak (had naught words), or those who were poor (had naught or nothing). It wasn't until later that it was used to describe behavior.

Gay started out as describing those who were happy and carefree. It was even used to describe a type of fabric. Now it is used primarily to refer to homosexual men (and sometimes women).

Today we have the politically correct who change descriptive terms with those they view as more favorable such as undocumented as opposed to illegal, equity and equality are becoming interchangeable, and pro-choice is used so the proper terms of abortion or murder of unborn children can be avoided.

And today we call our republic a democracy despite the two having more differences than they have similarities.

Master propagandists have been excellent at manipulating words and their meanings. The Marxist government of Russia called themselves the Union of Soviet Socialist Republics, wanting you to believe that the different socialist states that made up the new union were republics. They were states under dictatorial rule. China is named The

People's Republic of China. China is not a republic and is not of the people. North Korea is officially named the Democratic People's Republic of Korea. In this name, the closest descriptive term would be Democratic as North Korea is a dictatorship and democracy is a form of dictatorship leading to the oppressive form of dictatorship that is North Korea.

Absolutely, words do matter. Propagandists understand this. Marion Webster defines propagandist as a person who spreads ideas, facts, or allegations deliberately to further a cause or to damage an opposing cause. Propagandist connotates deceit or manipulation.

Joseph Goebbels, certainly a master propagandist said, "It would not be impossible to prove with sufficient repetition and a psychological understanding of the people concerned that a square is in fact a circle. They are mere words, and words can be molded until they clothe ideas and disguise."

Goebbels also said, "This is the secret of propaganda: Those who are to be persuaded by it should be completely immersed in the ideas of the propaganda, without ever noticing that they are being immersed in it."

In the modern United States, it is widely accepted that our nation is a democracy. That wasn't the intent of the founders. The founders understood that democracy is a form of dictatorship that will always lead to tyranny and destruction. The founders intended, and laid out the ground rules, for our nation to be a republic.

Remember the difference between republican and democratic forms of government? John Adams captured the essence of the difference when he described republic, "You have rights antecedent to all earthly governments; rights that cannot be repealed or restrained by human laws; rights derived from the Great Legislator of the Universe."

Nothing in our Constitution suggests that government is a grantor of rights. Instead, government is a protector of rights. Because government is a threat to our liberties, the framers used negative phrases against government throughout the Constitution such as shall not abridge, infringe, deny, disparage, and shall not be violated, nor be denied. In a republic the liberties of the people cannot be taken in any form from the people.

In a republican form of government, there is rule of law. All citizens, including government officials, are accountable to the same laws. Government power is limited and decentralized through a system of checks and balances, and federalism. Government intervenes in civil society to protect its citizens against force and fraud but does not intervene in the cases of peaceable, voluntary exchange. In a republic, Lady Justice is blindfolded and will never see race, color, gender, or political affiliation. In a democracy, Lady Justice sees all and adjudicates the way the majority or those in power tell her she must because of their desires. This is arbitrary law.

The founders clearly understood that in a democracy, the majority or those in power rule either directly or through elected representatives. As in a monarchy, the law is whatever that majority or those in power determines it to be. Laws do not necessarily represent reason, they represent power. The restraint is upon the individual instead of government. Unlike a republican form of government, in a democracy, rights are seen as privileges and permissions that are granted by government and can be rescinded by government. In a republic, the law, such as the United States Constitution, limits the power of government. In a democracy there are no limits placed on the power of government, it is whatever the majority or those in power declare it to be.

Chief Justice John Marshall observed, "Between a balanced republic and a democracy, the difference is like that between order and chaos."

The founders knew that a democracy would lead to the same kind of tyranny to which the colonies were subjected under King George III. Because of this, they gave us a republic with a Constitution that is filled with undemocratic mechanisms including the Electoral College. The purpose of the Electoral College was to prevent presidential elections from being totally controlled by large, heavily populated states and areas.

This is one of the reasons those calling for a democracy want to eliminate the Electoral College.

Do those who refer to our nation as a democracy share the republican values of our founders? Do they refer to us as a democracy simply out of ignorance, not understanding the differences between a republic and a democracy? Or is it a matter of preference, and they are using word manipulation to bring about the kind of tyranny or worse, feared by the founders?

Asked another way, do we want a republic where the powers of government are limited, or do we want a government where the majority or those in power have no limitations?

Do we want a republic where the liberties of the people are fully protected, or do we want a democracy where the majority or those in power can ration liberties as they believe is in their best interest?

A republic places limits on the government, the majority or those in power, and protects the liberties of the people from the government, the majority or those in power.

A republic must operate under the concept of rule of law. A democracy always operates under the concept of arbitrary law.

The more we refer to our republic as a democracy, the more power we give to the government, the majority or those in power. The more we refer to our republic as a democracy, the more we concede that our liberties can be rationed. The more we refer to our republic as a democracy, the more we accept that our law can be arbitrary and not based on rule of law, and any factor including political affiliation can be used as the factor for determining guilt or innocence.

It does matter if we are a republic or a democracy. It is the difference between freedom and liberty or dictatorship and tyranny.

Bibliography

Appleby, Joyce, Introduction and Notes, "Common Sense and Other Writings Thomas Paine", New York, Barnes &Noble Books, 2005

Barnett, Randy E., "Restoring the Lost Constitution", Princeton, New Jersey, Princeton University Press, 2014

Barnett, Randy E., "The Structure of Liberty Justice and the Rule of Law", Oxford, United Kingdom, Oxford University Press, 2014

Cooper, John Milton, Jr., "Woodrow Wilson A Biography", New York, Alfred a Knopf, 2009

Ferguson, Robert A., Introduction and Notes, "The Federalist", New York, Barnes & Nobel Books

Folsom, Burton, Jr., "New Deal or Raw Deal", New York, Threshold Editions, 2008

Harrison, T.R., "Hobbes, Locke, and Confusion's Masterpiece", New York, Cambridge University Press, 2003

Hillsdale College Politics Faculty, "The U.S. Constitution, a Reader", Hillsdale, Michigan, Hillsdale College Press, Thirteenth Printing 2021

Hobbes, Thomas, "Leviathan", Digireads.com Publishing 2017

Pestritto, Ronald J., "Woodrow Wilson and the Roots of Modern Liberalism", Lanham, Maryland, Rowman & Littlefield Publishers, Inc. 2005

Powell, Jim, "FDR's Folly", New York, Three Rivers Press, 2003

Schweikart, Larry, and Allen Michael, "A Patriot's History of the United States", New York, Penquin Group, 2004

Swanson, Mary-Elaine, "John Locke Philosopher of American Liberty", Ventura, California, Nordskog Publishing, 2012

Wood, Gordon S., The Creation of the American Republic 1176-1787", Chapel Hill, North Carolina, The University of North Carolina Press, 1998